SUN-KISSED COOKING

SUN-KISSED COOKING

Vegetables Front and Center

BROOKE WILLIAMSON
with JJ Goode
Photography by Huge Galdones

HARPER
An Imprint of HarperCollins*Publishers*

For my son, Hudson,
the greatest gift of my life.
You are my reason,
my constant motivation,
and my biggest inspiration,
every single day.

CONTENTS

TARTINE BOOK No 3
EVERYTHING I WANT TO EAT
mourad new moroccan
PLENTY MORE
JERUSALEM
FLAVORWALLA
BESTIA
SWEET
the wild table
PICKLES, PIGS & WHISKEY
BURMA
MATTY MATHESON
HOME STYLE COOKERY
HOG

INTRODUCTION

Each weekend morning of my childhood began the same way. I'd wake up early, grab a fuzzy blanket, and plant myself next to the wall heater, in front of the TV. I was only eight, but I wasn't watching cartoons—I was staring at hours upon hours of Graham, Julia, and Jacques. Only occasionally, during breaks between Julia making quiche lorraine and Jacques making lobster soufflé, did I flip the channel for my fix of Jem and the Holograms.

Once the credits rolled on *The Galloping Gourmet*, I'd turn off the TV and, hungry and inspired, get started on pancakes. I was alone those mornings. My night-owl parents were still dozing. My sister was at her dad's. I'd climb onto the kitchen counter and reach for the trusty *Betty Crocker Cookbook*. I'd find the dog-eared page for the pancake recipe and read it line by line, even though I'd already committed it to memory: *Do not overmix or pancakes will be tough. Cook until bubbly on top and dry around the edges.* Yep, still got it.

Pancakes weren't just the first dish I'd ever cooked—they were the first one I ever set out to master. After many attempts, I realized there was wisdom that wasn't contained in those instructions. Practice was required, for example, to get those crisp, buttery, brown edges and to know when to flip—when the surface had enough bubbles but not too many—to achieve the pancake version of medium-rare. I got good enough to experiment, heading out to our yard to forage for fruit for those pancakes. Growing up in LA, I was blessed with a yard with fruit trees and a garden, so I'd grab a cereal bowl and pick mulberries, figs, and strawberries, warm from the late-morning sun. Soon, the foraged fruit became each morning's inspiration. Pancakes were just the vehicle.

It was my mom's garden. She joined Graham, Julia, and Jacques as one of my culinary inspirations. She was the reason that, for the first fifteen years of my life, our family sat down to dinner at 6:30 p.m. sharp, five nights a week, with the TV off and the phone ignored. This was when my parents, my sister, and I talked about our day and our lives, when I could boast and bitch until I finished my food and my glass of milk and was excused from the table. Back then it didn't feel particularly important, but now I see how formative it was. The dinner table was where I first saw how food brought people together, where I formed enduring memories, and where I developed my hatred for drinking a straight glass of milk.

My mom was an adventurous cook who rarely made the same thing twice. She put so much effort into feeding us good, frequently elaborate meals—often with salad served at the end, like the traditional French family we are not. Every Sunday, she solicited our dinner requests for the week, not that she always took them. My dad asked for swordfish, lamb chops, and creamed chipped beef on toast (aka "shit on a shingle"). I wanted vegetables. To this day, my mom will tell you that I was a picky eater, but really, I just didn't care about protein. (The lone exception: the glorious chicken wings from the rotisserie place down the street.) Vegetables were special. Unlike steak and shrimp, acorn squash, for example, wasn't always at the market. I had to wait until fall for my mom—who was otherwise a health nut who stocked Grape-Nuts in the pantry and gave out raisins for Halloween—to roast it with butter and brown sugar. It felt naughty, like eating dessert for dinner.

I looked forward to artichokes in March for the simple, selfish reasons a kid from the East Coast looks forward to snow days in December. Because spring was when my mom would snip off the heads that grew like weeds in her garden and steam them for dinner. We'd each get an artichoke on our plate, and we'd pluck each leaf, dunk it in microwave-melted butter, and nibble the nub of flesh until they were gone. Then my mom would whisk them away to remove the chokes, gifting us the indulgent mouthful of heart that remained.

I grew up blessed in so many ways. By a yard with fruit trees (pomegranate, tangerine, kumquat!). By loving parents who supported my bouts of passion for various potential careers. I desperately wanted to be the first female Major League Baseball player, until I didn't. I wanted to ice skate in the Olympics, until I didn't. Both hippie New Yorkers turned Angelenos, my parents were patient, perhaps because they had managed to identify creative pursuits that they could turn into jobs. My mom worked as a fine artist, and spent her days throwing and firing pottery. My dad worked as a photographer, and spent late-night hours in a darkroom set up in our house that smelled, distinctly and fantastically, like chemical developer and weed.

The only enthusiasm I had that never wavered was for cooking. It blossomed slowly and steadily. First it was raiding the garden and making pancakes. Then it was watching my mom cook. Then it was spending my alone time experimenting by myself, making mostly messes and certainly nothing edible. At this point, butter and flour was my Play-Doh. When I realized cooking was morphing from hobby to passion, I knew I needed a way to get better at it. So my parents let me take weekend classes at a local culinary school, where the students were a mixture of housewives, husbands of exhausted housewives, and me, a girl who wasn't old enough to drive. At normal school, I withered. Here, I thrived. I listened. I practiced at home.

Back in those days (read that in your best old-lady voice), a preteen girl declaring her desire to become a professional chef was generally met with a scoff or, worse, a "that's cute." My intensity in the kitchen was driven in part by a desire to prove those people wrong. It was also driven by the feeling of accomplishment I got from making people happy. When I got my driver's license, I worked as a barista at a café on La Brea, and for the whole summer I brought in homemade cinnamon swirl coffee cake to sell. People bought it. People liked it! Real people, not just my parents.

In retrospect, I was also driven by my deep anxiety. At the time, we didn't know why I had "dizzy spells" and debilitating stomachaches that sent me home from school on a weekly basis. Doctors focused on identifying a physical cause, with futile CAT scans and blood draws that always came up empty. And so I learned to keep quiet, avoiding places and situations—planes, boats, movie theaters, driving on the freeway, public speaking, you name it—that made my palms sweat, my heart race, and my eyes blur as everything around me seemed to speed up. At the stove, however, I was at ease. And the better I got at cooking, the more at peace I felt.

I scored my first true restaurant gig when I was eighteen. I'd just quit college after my freshman year. And I'd just been fired—for the first and only time in my life—from a cocktail waitressing job, after refusing an advance from the owner (my bad). I found a job as a pastry assistant at Fenix, a restaurant by Michelin-starred chef Ken Frank, in what was once the Argyle Hotel on Sunset. I wasn't particularly interested in pastry, but that was the job they had to offer. The hours were long, the work physically demanding, but I was all in, exhilarated when I made it to the end of each exhausting day. As for my anxiety, I found comfort in being part of a team with a common task. People were relying on me. It could've felt like a trap, a surrender of control, but instead it felt like liberation.

When I wasn't working—or, let's be honest, partying, sometimes straight through to my 6 a.m. shift—I devoured cookbooks. (As a mediocre student, I think this was the first time I ever enjoyed reading.) I spent every moment of downtime at my job learning, thanks to a young cook who took me under his wing. A culinary school grad, he knew everything I didn't and walked me through it all—how to cut brunoise and debone quail and build veal stock. He asked for nothing in return. He just respected how much I cared.

When I eventually got the chance to move into the savory side of the kitchen, I made

sure to prove that I had been paying attention. I brought this hustle to my next job, at the iconic Michael's in Santa Monica, rising from hot apps cook to sous chef before I could legally drink in a kitchen whose bigwig alumni included Jonathan Waxman, Mark Peel, Nancy Silverton, and, coincidentally, my former boss Ken Frank.

My baby face and small stature made me stand out. When I was pictured alongside Sang Yoon, Michael's executive chef at the time, in the Santa Monica *Daily Breeze*, people took notice. *Who is this girl playing dress-up in chef's whites?* they must've thought. I always wondered whether without the novelty of my appearance I would've gotten a full review in *the L.A. Times* for my food at Zax when I was just twenty-two. In another review, written by Patric Kuh in *Los Angeles* magazine, there was a photo of me looking like a very tall toddler above the article's title: "Small Wonder." All that said, I deserved the praise. I was exacting. I busted my ass. And I was *good*.

When I was tasked (perhaps prematurely) with creating dishes and later entire menus, I looked for inspiration where I'd found it as a kid: From the fruit on trees, bushes, and vines. From the sweet, starchy roots and tubers peeking out of the dirt. From the flowering heads of cabbages and cauliflower, broccoli and romanesco. From the greens—leafy collards, bitter chicories, crisp Little Gem lettuces. Every plate began with produce. Every plate was determined by the season. This clarified my cooking, providing temptation (corn and tomatoes in the summer truly are irresistible) while imposing limitations (corn and tomatoes any other time are easy to resist).

The fruits and vegetables themselves helped guide me. If, say, stalks of asparagus were especially fat, they were just right for grilling (because they could be charred without losing their juicy snap) and bold, rich pairings. If they weren't, I might blanch them instead and keep the flavors light and bright. From there, it was about highlighting the vegetable's or fruit's best qualities, offsetting natural sweetness with acidity, bitterness with sweetness, and creaminess with crunch. Sometimes, a slab of steak, confited leg of duck, or octopus tentacle made an appearance alongside. More often, a little pork or salt cod or fish sauce wound up playing a background role, all in support of the stars of the show.

Then one day at Zax, I hired a guy named Nick Roberts. The beginning of my relationship with Nick was rom-com gold: He was an arrogant young cook who came into my kitchen thinking he knew more than I did. And perhaps he did. He had gone to culinary school. He was a great cook. He looked at me and thought, *Why is* she *my boss?* And at the time, I was thinking, *Because I hired you. That's why.* We disliked each other until we became friends. We were friends until we fell in love. Ultimately, we quit Zax to start a ragtag catering company. Soon, we were so big we needed to rent a space to cook out of, and once we found one, we ditched catering and instead opened our first restaurant. It turned out to be the first of many.

Around 2007, I got a call from a scout for a little show called *Top Chef*. At the time, the show's producers were seeking out potential female contestants to offset the hordes of men at the open auditions. For four years straight, I'd gotten calls from those scouts. Each time, I would consider the offer, but ultimately turn it down in one way or another, half filling out an application or half-assing an interview. I always had a good reason. I was pregnant with our son, Hudson. Or we were in the midst of opening a restaurant. In the back of my mind, of course, was another reason that I never quite acknowledged: that signing up for reality TV meant doing the unthinkable and relinquishing control, control I clutched like my life depended on it.

When I got the call again, I reached into my bag of excuses, but this time, I found myself grasping at air. Hudson was four, happy and settled and less demanding of my attention. Nick and I were running a couple of humming restaurants. He was an incredible dad and a talented chef who could pick up any slack on both the parenting and restaurant fronts. He told me to go for it. The only thing holding me back was fear. I thought about the opportunities I'd be giving up with yet another no, the ways I'd be failing our staff (the restaurant business is so tough, you need to take any chance to reduce the rate of failure). But mostly, I thought about Hudson. What kind of example would I set if I continued to let fear shape my life?

Now, had I known I'd have to ride in a helicopter, I might have thought again. (Tears streaming down my face, just before we took off, I asked, on mic, "Can we just wait five minutes until this Xanax kicks in?") But in a way, that was the point. I was confronting the idea that I didn't and couldn't know exactly what was headed my way. It was the right move. That year, I was honored to be runner-up to Kristen Kish. It was as life-changing as returning to the show four years later and winning the whole shebang.

Nowadays, I fly a lot, though not in helicopters and rarely without a gin and tonic. I do it because of the opportunities that taking that initial leap opened up for me. In addition to running a restaurant, I get to compete often on shows like *Bobby's Triple Threat* on Food Network. Going up against some of the best chefs around is the creative outlet I didn't know I needed. Keeps me sharp, too. Life still isn't always easy or pretty—I've had several full-blown panic attacks on live TV, though only those people closest to me could tell—but I'm no longer limited by what scares me. I know I'll get through it.

This revelation prepared me for what was to come. Because you don't always get to

choose whether or when to face your fears. Sometimes, the world decides that for you. The years since 2020 have been some of the hardest of my life. I'm certainly not alone in this, nor did I face anything close to the worst of it. Still, Nick and I shuttered three of our four restaurants, laying off people we'd worked with for more than a decade and whom we considered family.

As a break from a day of Zoom school, I decided to make Hudson run with me. I thought it might help him get the crazies out. It certainly helped me. After that, we ran often. He hated it, but it got him talking and helped us connect in a new way, an unexpected boon in an otherwise dark time. I usually asked questions about his life, but on one particularly long run, he turned the tables on me. He asked why I'd chosen the life I did, one that, as he saw it, was full of stress, financial uncertainty, and long, brutal workdays that didn't end even after I came home. He didn't get it. The only way I could explain it was that I couldn't imagine doing anything else. One of my great hopes is that he finds something that provides for him what cooking has for me.

Then two years ago, as I started writing this book, Nick and I decided, after twenty-one years together, to drop the romantic part of our relationship and just stick to being business partners, coparents, and best friends. It was incredibly difficult—and even worse, we had to tell our kind, empathetic, thoughtful, gorgeous, perfect fifteen-year-old boy.

After we finally did, a chef friend called to check on me. He asked how I was doing, and all I could think to say was, "I can't stop cooking." I didn't know what to say to Hudson. I didn't know how to help him cope with this new reality. For days, I stayed with him, feeding him pretty much nonstop. I made all his favorites: The Nutella crepes I've cooked for him nearly every Sunday since he was old enough to ask for them—I dread the day I no longer get this privilege. The bolognese he adored, layered in a lasagna—it was the best I've ever made. My desperation to make him happy, even for a moment, gave me *Top Chef* finale–level focus.

Of course, this storm of cooking was as much for me as it was for him. As my friend put it, for chefs, our aprons can be like suits of armor. In times of stress and sadness, he too cooked as a way to protect himself. The kitchen is where I express love. It's also where I've found calm in the chaos of my mind. It's where I feel confident and safe. Where I've learned I can only control the things I have control of.

In that sense, working on this cookbook during that particularly tumultuous moment in my life helped, too. I got to focus on cooking. I channeled my gratitude for this amazing gift, this strange superpower, into these recipes. I hope you love cooking from this book even half as much as I loved making it.

In it, I share the kind of food that makes me happy—laid-back dishes driven by the sun-kissed produce that have defined my lifetime in LA, full of color and texture and big flavors. I've organized the chapters in a way that reflects how I decide what to cook—basically, by asking myself, *What am I craving?*

Most often, I'm craving fruits and vegetables—maybe my mind is laser-focused on asparagus and artichokes because it's spring or on the sweet, starchy roots, like carrots, beets, and parsnips, that crowd farmers' markets in fall and winter. Fruits and vegetables are my Harry Styles; ingredients like pancetta and duck fat, shrimp shells and fish sauce are the band, the keyboard, drums, and bass. Produce is the foundation of every recipe in this book, not because I'm on a quest for everyone to eat more plants, but because I want to showcase how delicious fruits and vegetables are when they receive the same consideration and attention usually bestowed upon meat.

After the craving strikes, the mood determines in which direction to take that inspiring ingredient. Say I'm craving corn. On hot summer days, for instance, I want it grilled on the cob or I want those perfect raw kernels in a bright salad (page 89) or that gorgeous sweetness infused into creamy, wobbly panna cotta (page 228). Yet toward the end of the season, when nights turn chilly, I can't wait to make heftier, cozier food like creamy, steamy corn chowder (page 74) or savory corn pancakes laced with bacon. And just because summer ends doesn't mean my corn cravings do. Fresh corn might not be at its best come fall, but sweet, custardy cornbread (page 80) made with cornmeal and canned creamed corn really does hit the spot, especially when it's slathered with date butter.

My recipes give you all the instructions you need to make some of my favorite dishes, but look closer, and you'll see that they're also full of tools and lessons—fun ones, I promise. This means you can make my Carrot-Glazed Carrots with Coconut Milk and Seedy Za'atar Granola (page 205), or you can just borrow the technique of cooking carrots in carrot juice or make the crunchy topping to bring a little textural intrigue to your own roasted carrots. You can serve my asparagus with fennel-anchovy dressing (page 28), or you can just nab the bright, crisp dressing or repurpose the blanching method, which is the perfect way to accentuate the crispy, juicy spears.

Along with a repository of drizzles and dressings and breadcrumbs, the recipes also feature an arsenal of flavor-fortifying pantry ingredients—Espelette pepper and porcini powder, salt cod and chorizo, miso and black garlic—that will supercharge your everyday cooking. It's all in the service of taking produce from the side of the plate to the center of the table.

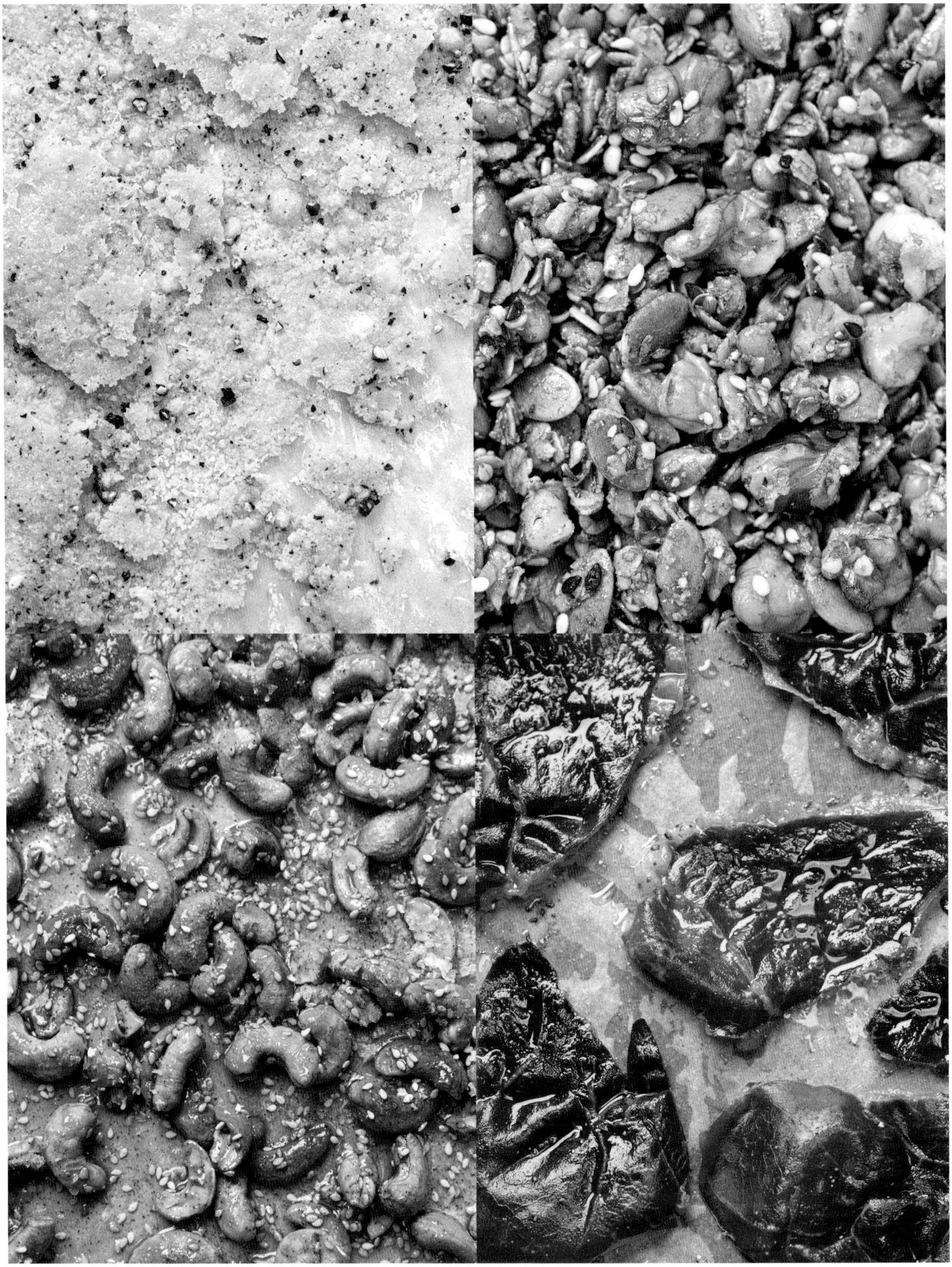

PANTRY
How to Up Your Game

This book is full of instructions for making some really awesome food, if I do say so myself. But the recipes are also blueprints that reflect how I think when I create vegetable- and fruit-focused food that commands attention.

Each dish is wildly different, but look closer and you'll see that they share certain principles, ingredients, and components. In this section, I call out the ones I use again and again in my cooking that you can work into your own, whether you make each recipe in full or just borrow bits and pieces. Here, I'll briefly introduce you to some of the pantry items, dressings, breadcrumbs, drizzles, and sprinkles you can apply to simply prepared produce to make it taste amazing. I hope you'll treat them as a sort of arsenal to draw from whenever you're cooking what caught your eye at the market.

One more thing: While I tried to dial in the amounts of salt, acid, herbs, etc., so each dish tastes great, I encourage you to find your own sweet spot, always tasting before you serve and adjusting as you'd like.

Acidity

In just about every dish I make, I employ some form of acid to balance the inherent sweetness of great produce and/or underscore natural acidity. For bright acidity, there's fresh fruit, of course—I'm thinking lemon, lime, and orange, but also Meyer lemon, an especially fragrant citrus common in California but available elsewhere and worth seeking out. Pomegranate seeds, cherry tomatoes, and other tart fruits are great for adding acid in little bursts throughout a dish.

For a punchier acidity, I look to rice vinegar (delicate, with a slight sweetness), red wine vinegar and sherry vinegar (sharper and more pungent), whole-grain mustard (tangy, with a bonus nose-tickle), and pomegranate molasses (dark and tangy, with a touch of sweetness).

Sometimes a splash of vinegar or a squeeze of lemon will do; sometimes I'll whip up a dressing to coat endive and apples (the sherry vinaigrette on page 133), broccoli and potatoes (the curry-spiked vinaigrette on page 171), or Little Gems and persimmon (the zippy, creamy tahini green goddess on page 136).

Sweetness

Just as acid balances sweetness and bolsters natural acidity, sweetness offsets acidity and reinforces natural sweetness. Sometimes, that sweetness comes from sugar—granulated white if my only goal is sweetness, or products like brown sugar, honey, and maple syrup if I want to add flavor as well. In other instances, I choose ingredients that are sweet by nature—dried apricots (page 193) to underscore the sweetness of parsnips, caramelized onions (page 199) to accentuate the sugars in honeynut squash risotto, tangerine and orange segments (page 130) to balance the bitterness of treviso, crab (page 68) to add a luxurious sea-sweet element to tomato salad.

Fat

Fat does so much for food. It carries flavor—in other words, when it's around, flavors are a little bigger and bolder. (Too much fat, though, can mute flavor.) It also helps create textures and flavors we love. Creaminess, caramelization, crunch, they all require fat.

Each source of fat has its own character. Olive oil is grassy and slightly, delightfully bitter. Butter is round and luxurious. Bacon fat (page 193) is smoky and porky, bold enough to stand up to and properly boost the flavor of parsnips. Duck fat (page 189) is aromatic and, uh, duck-y, its delicate pleasures a perfect match for the quiet earthiness of potatoes. A little cream (page 147) serves as a megaphone for the mushrooms and marsala in an irresistible gravy. Feta (page 57) in snap pea salad provides creamy zing, and whipped ricotta (page 67) means the flavor of tomatoes slow-roasted with saffron, fennel seeds, and thyme lingers even longer on your palate.

Yet oils and animals aren't the only sources of fat. Chunks of avocado (page 48) in fresh, zippy soba salad, tahini (page 97) drizzled on blistered shishito peppers, and cashews (page 165) inside (and on top of) cabbage rolls are just a few other ways to wield flavor-enhancing fat.

Bitterness

An unsung hero in so much memorable food, bitterness can add intrigue and pull dishes back from the brink of too sweet. So many ingredients have a natural bitterness that's part of what makes them so craveable—think walnuts (page 34), which I toss with recently picked asparagus and pecorino, and pomegranate seeds (page 64), which I sprinkle on tomato-bread salad.

Sometimes, the key is manipulating an ingredient's bitterness, toning it down so it won't overwhelm a dish, which is why I grill the treviso on page 130, or bumping it up to balance other elements, like the charred onions on page 64 and the charred red cabbage on page 182.

Fresh Herbs

When in doubt, add herbs. Herbs like cilantro, mint, and parsley add color and freshness that can provide lift to heavy dishes and double down on the punch of light, bright dishes. Hardier herbs like thyme, sage, and rosemary contribute an aromatic quality that produce rarely has by itself. I'm a fan of all herbs, except curly parsley, which is all frill and no flavor. If you're garnishing a ham in the 1970s, sure, use it. Otherwise, flat-leaf only, please.

Texture

We all know contrast keeps things interesting—that's why sweet and salty, and tart and sweet make such good pairings. Yet contrasting textures, which chefs frequently use to add excitement, are typically overlooked when we're cooking at home.

Sometimes, it's just about thoughtfully choosing fruits and vegetables—for example, crisp Little Gem lettuce and soft, juicy persimmon (page 136), or kohlrabi and Asian pear (page 134) in a collard green slaw. Sometimes, produce provides the crispness and your goal is to provide the creaminess (see the watermelon salad with whipped feta on page 113).

Often, fruits and vegetables with soft, luscious, juicy qualities—cooked carrots, ripe tomatoes, tender roasted cauliflower—yearn for crispness and crunch. Doing so can be as simple as scattering on nuts, breadcrumbs, pumpkin seeds, and the like. Or you can bake prosciutto to a crackerlike crisp (page 195) to pair with roasted beets, sprinkle za'atar granola (page 205) on glazed carrots, or make tortilla crumble (page 90) to coat roasted baby corn. And because crunch and fat are typically a package deal, it's no

surprise that a lot of my favorite sources of crunch come with some bonus flavor-giving fat—think fried shallots (page 31) sprinkled on blanched asparagus dressed in punchy anchovy dressing, and buttery breadcrumbs (page 99) on spaghetti with zucchini.

Heat

The heat from chiles has this magical ability to both enhance and rein in flavor. Take, for example, a sauce headlined by honey. Without the heat of chiles, not only could the sauce lack excitement and overall punch, it could also taste out of balance, because heat tempers sweetness. I use chiles often and in many varieties, because each brings unique character.

Fresh green chiles (page 85) have a grassy sharpness that cuts the sweetness of the summer corn in savory pancakes, and fresh red chiles (page 182), slightly sweeter and fruitier, bring the perfect sting to the riff on Vietnamese nước chấm I use to glaze charred red cabbage. Calabrian chiles (page 37), packed in oil and sold whole or crushed to a coarse paste, deliver their savory heat—to me the flavor clocks in somewhere between fresh and dried chiles—to the buttery sauce I serve with grilled artichokes and braised greens with mortadella, an Italian chile fueling two (vaguely) Italian dishes.

Dried chiles come in endless varieties and offer another dimension of flavor and a different sort of tongue-tingling heat—less sharp, more slow-burning. There's piment d'Espelette, a powdered dried Basque chile whose bright, fruity heat I love with cooked tomato. There's floral Kashmiri chili powder (page 167), a variety more common in Indian cooking, in cabbage rolls stuffed with lentils and cashews. And there's gochugaru (page 148), Korean chile flakes whose fruity, smoky flavor enlivens boldly flavored vegetables like mushrooms. The good news is, they're all readily available in good markets and online.

Of course, everyone has their own particular tolerance for heat, so feel free to adjust the amounts to your taste.

Salt

I think we all know how important this elemental seasoning is to great food. Still, I've found that the biggest difference between the food of pro cooks and home cooks is how much they use. We pros use so much more.

The fear of oversalting—a valid one, since at a certain point there's no going back—

keeps home cooks from using enough to fully highlight all those other flavors. The recipes in this book guide you to a delicious place, but of course, everyone has their own happy zone when it comes to saltiness. So before you serve, always taste and adjust, gradually adding more until you reach a point where the flavors seem more vibrant but before saltiness dominates.

There are many sources of salt in this book, many of which (fish sauce, miso, cheese, etc.) offer other flavors and qualities, too (see umami, below). The two types of salt I use deserve a moment of explanation. One is flaky sea salt, which I sprinkle on certain dishes right before serving for its bright salinity and crunch. Maldon is the most common brand, but any delicate flakes will do. The other is kosher salt. That's the workhorse. That's the type most chefs use to season while cooking. I use Diamond Crystal kosher salt, because I like the way it feels between my fingers. I recommend finding a brand that suits you, though keep in mind that Morton kosher salt, another common brand, is denser, which means it'll add almost twice as much salt per teaspoon compared to Diamond Crystal. Sticking to one brand is smart, too—switching means your pinches deliver unpredictable amounts.

Umami

When I'm trying to impress a judge with a single bite of food or looking to serve friends a meal that tastes OMG SO GOOD, umami is on my mind. To describe umami, known as the "fifth taste," I like to think about ingredients that provide it, then imagine stripping away the other four tastes—salty, sweet, sour, bitter. What's left for, say, chicken stock, fish sauce, Parmesan, miso, and the like is this intense craveability, this ethereal mouth-filling sensation of, well, deliciousness, which enhances everything else. Recognizing and using various sources of umami will up your game in the kitchen. It's like classy cheating. Here are some of my favorites.

I often look to mushrooms—from cooked fresh shiitake to pulverized dried porcini, which you can buy already powdered or make using a spice grinder—and their cousins, truffles. (Sabatino brand truffle zest is inexpensive and tasty.) Stock is another thing you'll see often in my cooking—shellfish stock (page 106) in fideos with summer vegetables, reduced chicken stock (page 33) for a mustard-spiked sauce for grilled asparagus, even stock made from bacon (page 45) for favas. You can buy it or make it by following the approximately one million recipes for stock that have already been written.

Sealife brims with umami. Anchovies, fish sauce (including Italian colatura, which I like to think of as anchovy juice), seaweed, katsuobushi (dried cured bonito flakes)—the list goes on. That's why I add salt cod (page 74) to my corn chowder and infuse butter with shrimp shells (page 37). Meat, too, and primarily pork, infuses dishes with umami, which is why I add guanciale (cured jowl) (page 70) to tomatoey fregola, chorizo to honey (for the figs on page 94) and to a stew with chickpeas (page 51), and mortadella (page 129) to braised greens. Fermentation frequently produces umami, as it does in fish sauce and Parmesan (the cheese begins as milk fermented by lactic acid bacteria), miso (fermented soybeans), and black garlic (fermented garlic).

With umami, the vibe is the more the merrier. Parm and cooked tomatoes work so well together to make umami explosions for the same reason black garlic and button mushrooms (page 158) and shiitakes and oyster sauce (page 161) do.

Double (and Triple) Threats

Here's where things get extra fun—when you choose ingredients or whip up a sauce, sprinkle, or other concoction that delivers several delicious elements at once.

I've mentioned some of these multitalented ingredients before. Anchovy, miso, and Parm all bring salt *and* umami. Sweet fish sauce drizzle (page 190) and prosciutto baked to a crackerlike crisp (page 195) do, too, adding sweetness to the mix in the case of the former and texture in the case of the latter.

Dressings add acid, fat, and salt, and sometimes more. I love to sneak texture into dressings, whether that's thinly sliced green beans (page 148) for crispness, black lentils (page 63) for a delicate bite, tangerine segments (page 130) for juicy mouthfuls, or toasted pumpkin seeds (page 186) for a touch of crunch.

Virtually every sauce and dressing in this book hits deliciousness from multiple fronts—romesco (page 84) and salsa macha (page 78), chipotle ranch (page 90) and red chile garlic sauce (page 167) all bring fat, acid, salt, sweetness, and heat in different proportions. Hibiscus ponzu (page 48) is a wallop of acid and umami, and beet-pickled eggs (page 171) deliver sweetness, tang, and fat.

You'll find breadcrumbs—butter-toasted, lemon zest–sprinkled (page 101); tossed with oil, baked, and spiked with the dusky North African chile paste harissa (page 170)—that you can tweak however you'd like. Add a last-minute flurry of Parmesan along with the lemon zest in the former, and the result would go great on roasted broccoli. Swap Calabrian chiles or anchovies for harissa in the latter, and ditto.

There's a small arsenal of sprinkles made with nuts and herbs or spices that exist somewhere between Italian gremolata and Egyptian dukkah. One made from pine nuts, sesame seeds, cumin, and coriander adds crunch and reinforces the flavors of cauliflower tossed with spiced tomato sauce (page 177). Another made from pistachios, parsley, and lemon zest (page 193) lightens bacon-roasted parsnips. Farro cooked in carrot juice gets crunch, fat, and extra umami from a jumble of parsley, roasted sunflower seeds, and sizzled chicken skin (page 207).

The butter (page 37) I pair with grilled artichokes is infused with shrimp shells (umami!), mixed with capers (salt!), Calabrian chile (heat!), lemon (acid), and parsley (herbs!). That's a lot of good.

ARTICHOKES AND ASPARAGUS

So Very Spring

Artichoke-and-Crab Dip Toasts

Artichoke dip is always a winner, but with a few tweaks, it can be next-level delicious. For me, that means going heavy on the artichokes and using the best and most neutrally flavored jarred or canned hearts (no vinegar or dried herbs, please) I can find. Real Parm, lemon zest, and some Worcestershire provide a check on the gluttonous creaminess, and fresh lump crab brings a touch of salinity and opulence. I pile it all on toasts and pop them into the oven to bubble and brown.

MAKES 8 LOADED TOASTS

For the dip

1 (14-ounce) can artichoke hearts, drained and chopped
1 (8-ounce) package cream cheese, at room temp
1 cup shredded Jack cheese
½ cup mayonnaise
½ cup finely grated Parmesan cheese
2 teaspoons Worcestershire sauce
1½ teaspoons kosher salt, plus more as needed
¼ teaspoon freshly ground black pepper, plus more as needed
¼ teaspoon red chile flakes
3 garlic cloves, grated on a Microplane
2 scallions, thinly sliced
Handful of fresh parsley, chopped
Finely grated zest of 1 lemon
8 ounces lump crabmeat, picked over for shells

For the toasts

8 slices good crusty bread (about 1 inch thick)
Extra-virgin olive oil, for drizzling
½ teaspoon kosher salt
Pinch of freshly ground black pepper
4 small radishes, thinly sliced (a mandoline helps), soaked in ice water for 15 minutes, and drained
2 scallions, thinly sliced on an angle
Juice of ½ lemon
Flaky sea salt, like Maldon
A few lemon wedges, for serving

Make the dip

Combine the artichoke hearts, cream cheese, Jack cheese, mayonnaise, Parmesan, Worcestershire, salt, pepper, chile flakes, garlic, scallions, parsley, and lemon zest in a large bowl and stir well. Add the crab and fold it in gently to keep the chunks nice and big. Season to taste with salt and pepper. (The dip will keep in an airtight container in the fridge for up to 1 day.)

Make the toasts

Preheat the oven to 400°F.

Put the bread on a large baking sheet, drizzle each slice with olive oil, and lightly season with salt and pepper. Bake, flipping each slice halfway through, until they're lightly toasted, about 8 minutes.

Remove from the oven and top the toasts generously with the dip (seriously, don't be shy). Return them to the oven and bake, rotating the baking sheet once halfway through, until the dip is bubbling and the top is browned in spots, about 20 minutes. (If you'd like more color, give it a minute or two under the broiler.) Let the toasts cool slightly (that dip is lava-hot!).

Meanwhile, put the radishes, scallions, lemon juice, a splash of olive oil, and a sprinkle of flaky salt in a small bowl and toss to combine.

Top the warm toasts with the radish mixture and serve with lemon wedges on the side.

Artichoke Cakes with Horseradish Celery Root Rémoulade

Everyone knows there's no substitute for crab cakes. That said, these are kind of a great substitute for crab cakes. Part of the joy of a crab cake is that crisp-on-the-outside, lush-on-the-inside quality. And that's just what you get from these beauties, plus the lovely texture of artichoke hearts and hearty barley. When I eat them with crunchy, creamy, nose-tickling celery root rémoulade and a splash of sweet, spicy hot sauce (see page 27), I'll say that, even as a hard-core crab lover, I don't miss a thing.

SERVES 4 TO 6

For the rémoulade

¼ cup mayonnaise
¼ cup crème fraîche
1 tablespoon prepared white horseradish
1 tablespoon lemon juice
1 tablespoon chopped capers
1 teaspoon Dijon mustard
1 teaspoon whole-grain mustard
½ teaspoon kosher salt
¼ teaspoon freshly ground black pepper
¼ teaspoon celery seed
¼ teaspoon piment d'Espelette or red chile flakes
5 cornichons, finely chopped, plus 1 tablespoon of brine from the jar
Big pinch of chopped fresh parsley
Small pinch of chopped fresh tarragon
12 ounces celery root, peeled and cut into thin matchsticks

For the cakes

2 celery stalks, finely diced (about ½ cup)
1 small red onion, finely diced (about ½ cup)
4 garlic cloves, minced
1 tablespoon extra-virgin olive oil
1 (14-ounce) can artichoke hearts, drained and chopped
1 cup cooked barley
1 cup drained cooked or canned chickpeas, coarsely smashed
⅓ cup mayonnaise
1 large egg, lightly beaten, plus 2 for breading
Finely grated zest and juice of 1 lemon
1½ teaspoons kosher salt
¼ teaspoon freshly ground black pepper
½ teaspoon ground fenugreek or curry powder
½ teaspoon garlic powder
¼ teaspoon celery seed
¼ teaspoon piment d'Espelette or red chile flakes
3¼ cups panko breadcrumbs
1 cup all-purpose flour
Neutral oil, like canola, plus more if needed
Flaky sea salt, like Maldon

(continued)

Make the rémoulade

Stir together all of the rémoulade ingredients except for the celery root in a large bowl, then stir in the celery root. (The rémoulade will keep in an airtight container in the fridge for a day or two.)

Make the cakes

Preheat the oven to 250°F.

Cook the celery, onions, and garlic in 1 tablespoon of olive oil in a medium pan over medium heat, stirring occasionally, until soft but not browned, about 5 minutes. Transfer to a large bowl and let them cool slightly.

Add the artichoke hearts, barley, chickpeas, mayonnaise, 1 egg, the lemon zest, lemon juice, salt, pepper, fenugreek, garlic powder, celery seed, and piment d'Espelette to the bowl and stir to combine. Add ¾ cup of the breadcrumbs and mix well.

Pop the bowl in the fridge for 10 minutes so the breadcrumbs soak up some of the moisture. Then form the mixture into 5 cakes that are about 3 inches in diameter and 2 inches thick. Put them on a plate and refrigerate until the cakes firm up a bit, about 30 minutes.

Scatter ½ cup of the remaining breadcrumbs over a baking sheet. Put the flour, the remaining 2 eggs, and remaining 2 cups breadcrumbs in separate shallow bowls; lightly beat the eggs. Bread the cakes one at a time: Add them first to the flour and turn to completely coat, then add them to the egg, and then the bowl of breadcrumbs, patting to help them adhere. As they're done, transfer them to the breadcrumb-covered baking sheet and refrigerate until you're ready to fry them, up to 6 hours.

Line a second baking sheet with paper towels. Heat about ¾ inch of oil in a large heavy-bottomed skillet over medium-high heat until it shimmers. Working in batches to avoid crowding, add the cakes to the hot oil and cook, flipping once, until golden brown on both sides, 3 minutes per side. As they're done, transfer the cakes to the paper towel–lined baking sheet, immediately sprinkle with flaky salt, and pop them in the oven to keep warm. Repeat with the remaining cakes, adding more oil between batches to maintain a ¾-inch depth, if necessary, and letting it heat up before adding the cakes.

Serve the cakes topped with a generous crown of rémoulade.

Note: These cakes also taste fantastic with romesco (page 84) or the hot sauce that follows.

Pickled Habanero Hot Sauce

MAKES ABOUT 3 CUPS

2 cups diced (about ½ inch), peeled carrots
1 cup apple cider vinegar
½ cup water
⅓ cup white sugar
2 tablespoons kosher salt
3 garlic cloves, peeled
½ cup diced yellow onion
½ to 1 fresh habanero chile, stemmed

Bring a medium pot of water to a boil over high heat, add the carrots, and cook, stirring, until fully tender, 8 to 10 minutes. Drain the carrots well.

Meanwhile, combine the vinegar, water, sugar, and salt in a quart container and stir to dissolve the sugar and salt. Add the garlic, onions, habanero, and cooked carrots. Stir well, then cover and refrigerate for 24 hours.

After 24 hours, drain the solids, reserving the pickling liquid. Put the solids in a blender and blend until very smooth, gradually adding just enough of the reserved liquid as necessary to achieve a smooth puree. If any seeds remain, strain the mixture before using.

The hot sauce keeps in an airtight container in the fridge for up to 3 weeks.

Blanched Asparagus with Fennel-Anchovy Dressing and Fried Shallots

While asparagus takes well to cream and butter, I also look for ways to keep this spring delicacy clean and light. Blanching—a quick dunk in salty boiling water, then a plunge in ice water—brings out the vegetable's juicy snap, and the dressing is tart and refreshing, with lots of lemon, anchovy for umami, and crisp raw fennel. Fried shallots, homemade or store-bought, offer a little fat and crunch.

SERVES 4

For the dressing

¼ cup finely minced fennel bulb, fronds reserved for garnish
3 tablespoons red wine vinegar
1 tablespoon thinly sliced fresh chives
1 tablespoon honey
1 tablespoon minced preserved lemon rind
1 tablespoon colatura (Italian anchovy sauce)
1 teaspoon Dijon mustard
¼ teaspoon Aleppo pepper or red chile flakes
Finely grated zest of 1 Meyer lemon
Juice of 2 Meyer lemons
1 large garlic clove, grated on a Microplane

For the asparagus

Kosher salt
2 bunches thick asparagus
Flaky sea salt, like Maldon
Extra-virgin olive oil, for drizzling
¼ cup Fried Shallots (recipe follows)

Make the dressing

Combine all the dressing ingredients in a medium bowl and stir well. Set aside.

Make the asparagus

Bring a large pot of water to a boil and salt it heavily so it tastes like the sea. Fill a large bowl with ice and water.

Snap off and discard the tough bottoms of the asparagus. Use a vegetable peeler to peel all but the top couple of inches. Add the asparagus to the boiling water and cook until bright green and tender but still crisp, about 1 minute. Transfer the asparagus to the ice water and let cool completely.

Drain and dry the asparagus thoroughly. Transfer to a serving plate (I like to make a little pyramid). Give the dressing a quick whisk, then spoon it over the asparagus. Lightly sprinkle with flaky salt and drizzle generously with olive oil. Garnish with the fried shallots and a small handful of fennel fronds and serve.

(continued)

Fried Shallots

MAKES ABOUT 1 CUP

6 medium shallots
2 cups neutral oil, like canola
¼ teaspoon kosher salt

Slice the shallots into very thin rings (a mandoline makes your life much easier). Shoot for the thickness of a quarter. Use your fingers to separate the layers of the shallot into individual rings.

Combine the shallots and oil in a small saucepan, set it over medium-low heat, and wait until they begin to sizzle, 4 to 6 minutes. Cook, stirring frequently, until the bubbling subsides and the shallots turn golden brown, 20 to 25 minutes more.

Strain the shallots, reserving the tasty oil for another purpose, and spread them on paper towels to drain excess oil. Immediately sprinkle with the salt and let cool completely.

The fried shallots will keep in an airtight container (with a square of paper towel at the bottom) in a cool, dark place for up to 4 days.

Charred Asparagus with Buttery Parmesan Mustard Sauce

The high heat of a grill or skillet makes asparagus taste even more like asparagus, concentrating its grassy flavor. It's the perfect way to treat thick spears, because they can pick up plenty of char without sacrificing their crunch. The bold result can stand up to this rich, punchy sauce of reduced chicken stock dosed with butter, mustard, and Parm.

SERVES 4 TO 6

2 bunches thick asparagus
3 tablespoons extra-virgin olive oil
1½ teaspoons kosher salt, plus more as needed
¼ teaspoon freshly ground black pepper, plus more as needed
1 small shallot, minced
1 cup unsalted chicken stock
1 tablespoon whole-grain mustard
2 teaspoons sherry vinegar
2 tablespoons unsalted butter
Juice of ½ lemon
2 tablespoons finely grated Parmesan cheese, plus more for garnish
Thinly sliced fresh chives, for garnish

Snap off and discard the tough bottoms of the asparagus. Use a vegetable peeler to peel the bottom third or so.

Prepare a grill, preferably charcoal, to cook with high heat. Alternatively, set a grill pan over high heat. Toss the asparagus with 2 tablespoons of the olive oil and the salt and pepper. When the grill or pan is good and hot, add the asparagus and cook, flipping occasionally with tongs, until nicely charred but still snappy, 4 to 6 minutes. Set aside.

Heat the remaining 1 tablespoon olive oil in a small saucepan over medium-low heat until it shimmers. Add the shallot and cook, stirring occasionally, until soft but not browned, 3 to 4 minutes. Stir in the stock, mustard, and vinegar and bring to a strong simmer. Cook, stirring occasionally, until reduced by about half, 6 to 8 minutes. Remove the pan from the heat. Whisk in the butter and lemon juice, then the Parm. Season to taste with salt.

Put the asparagus in a serving bowl. Pour on the mustard sauce, sprinkle with chives and more Parmesan and pepper, and serve.

Raw Asparagus Salad with Pancetta, Walnuts, and Pecorino

If you have access to freshly plucked asparagus, whether the plucker was the farmer running a stand or you crouched in your garden, take a bite. It's grassy, it's earthy, and it's *sweet*—a quality we don't often associate with asparagus. To celebrate those lucky moments, I tumble raw crisp slivers with ingredients designed to highlight that special sweetness and round out the rawness—toasty walnuts, salty pancetta and pecorino, and lots of lemon.

SERVES 3 OR 4

6 ounces pancetta, cut into ½-inch cubes
¼ cup extra-virgin olive oil, plus a splash for the pancetta
1 heaping cup raw walnuts
1 pound asparagus (spears of thin to medium thickness are ideal here)
½ cup coarsely grated Pecorino Romano cheese
1½ teaspoons freshly ground black pepper
1 teaspoon flaky sea salt, like Maldon
¼ teaspoon red chile flakes
Finely grated zest of 1 lemon
¼ cup lemon juice
1 small shallot, minced
Handful of parsley, coarsely chopped
Handful of basil leaves (I like opal basil here), thinly sliced at the last minute

Put the pancetta and a splash of oil in a small skillet. Cook over medium heat, stirring occasionally, until the fat renders out and the pancetta is crisp, 5 to 7 minutes. Transfer the pancetta to a large bowl using a slotted spoon. Pour out the tasty fat, reserving it for another purpose.

Add the walnuts to the skillet and toast over medium heat, stirring occasionally, until fragrant, about 3 minutes. Give them a rough chop and transfer to the bowl with the pancetta.

Snap off and discard the tough bottoms of the asparagus. Slice the asparagus thinly (shoot for ⅛ inch) on an angle. Add the asparagus to the bowl, then add the walnuts, pecorino, pepper, flaky salt, red chile flakes, lemon zest, lemon juice, shallot, parsley, and basil. Toss to combine and serve on a platter.

Grilled Artichokes with Chile, Capers, and Lemony, Garlicky Shrimp Butter

Give me a steamed artichoke with melted butter for dipping and my Californian heart is full. Yet when I have the time, I up the ante, hitting tender 'chokes with a little char to add another dimension and upgrading the butter by infusing with a wildly underutilized ingredient: shrimp shells. Cooking them gently coaxes out a toasty crustacean flavor, and the addition of lemon, capers, and chile gives that butter sauce a thrilling punch.

SERVES 4 TO 6

For the artichokes

2 lemons, halved
Kosher salt
4 medium to large artichokes (preferably globe)

For the shrimp butter

2 sticks (1 cup) unsalted butter
4 ounces shrimp shells and/or heads (from about 1 pound shrimp)
4 garlic cloves, smashed and peeled
1 tablespoon drained capers
1 teaspoon crushed Calabrian chile
½ teaspoon kosher salt, plus more as needed
Small handful of parsley, chopped
Juice of ½ lemon
2 tablespoons extra-virgin olive oil
½ teaspoon freshly ground black pepper

Prepare the artichokes

Bring a large pot of water to a boil. Squeeze the lemons into the water (throw the rinds in, too) and salt it heavily so it tastes like the sea. Meanwhile, trim the artichokes by lopping off the top third. Use scissors to snip off any sharp leaf tips. Trim all but 2 inches of the stem, then peel the stem with a peeler or paring knife. Add the artichokes and a plate to weigh them down, then cover and cook at an aggressive simmer until you can easily pierce the stems with a small sharp knife, 30 to 40 minutes.

Stand the artichokes stem-side up on kitchen towels to drain. Let them cool to room temperature. At this point, you can stick them in the fridge overnight before serving, if you like.

Make the butter

Put the butter and shrimp shells in a medium saucepan over medium heat. When the butter has melted, reduce the heat to medium-low and cook, stirring occasionally, for 8 minutes to extract the flavor from the shells. Reduce the heat to low, stir in the garlic, and cook for 5 minutes to extract its flavor.

(continued)

Strain the mixture, discarding the solids, then return it to the pan. Stir in the capers, Calabrian chile, salt, parsley, and lemon juice and keep warm.

Prepare a grill to cook with high heat. Alternatively, set a grill pan over high heat.

Quarter the artichokes lengthwise through the stem. Scrape out the choke (the fuzzy, spiky part in the middle) with a small spoon.

Brush the artichokes with the olive oil and season lightly with salt and pepper. When the grill or pan is good and hot, add the artichokes and cook, turning once, until the cut sides are lightly charred, about 2 minutes per side.

Transfer to a serving plate, spoon on the butter, and serve.

Note: I never buy peeled shrimp. First of all, shell-on shrimp are less expensive. Second, they come with a big bonus: Strip off those shells and you have a game-changing, flavor-packed ingredient in your back pocket (or in your freezer, if you want to get literal). Same goes, by the way, for crab and lobster shells, even after they're cooked! So start your own collection or ask your friendly fishmonger if any of their stash is for sale.

PEAS AND PODS

Delicious Fresh, Frozen, and Dried

Braised Butter Beans and Fennel, Anchovies, Tomato, and Pernod

For our tenth anniversary, Nick surprised me with a food-filled trip to New Orleans. One of our favorite meals was at Willie Mae's Scotch House, where the phenomenal fried chicken was almost as memorable as the simple braised butter beans, cooked forever to a creamy, fantastic mush. This California girl had never heard of butter beans (which I've since learned are the same as lima beans), but she sure loved them.

Ever since then, I've been cooking with butter beans at home, and here you'll find one of my favorite ways to eat them. I double down on their creamy texture with a little crème fraîche and butter and add roasted fennel for texture and Pernod to underscore that fennel flavor. For acidity, I sneak in sun-dried tomatoes, which I don't think I've used since the '90s but which hold their shape nicely here.

SERVES 4

1 pound dried butter beans (aka lima beans), soaked in water to cover overnight and drained
2 large fennel bulbs (about 1½ pounds)
Extra-virgin olive oil
Kosher salt
6 garlic cloves, thinly sliced
6 medium leeks, white and pale green parts only, halved lengthwise, cleaned, and thinly sliced
½ cup sliced (½-inch) drained oil-packed sun-dried tomatoes
1 generous tablespoon finely chopped fresh thyme leaves
10 oil-packed anchovy fillets, drained
½ cup Pernod
4 cups unsalted chicken stock
2 teaspoons crushed Calabrian chile
¼ cup crème fraîche
½ stick (4 tablespoons) unsalted butter
2 teaspoons piment d'Espelette or crushed Calabrian chile
Handful of parsley, chopped
Finely grated zest and juice of 2 lemons, plus more juice to taste
Freshly ground black pepper

Combine the drained beans in a medium pot with enough fresh water to cover them by about 3 inches. Bring to a boil, reduce the heat to maintain a gentle simmer, and cover with a lid set ajar. Cook, stirring occasionally, until tender but with a slight bite, about 45 minutes. Drain the beans, reserving a cup or so of the cooking liquid.

Meanwhile, preheat the oven to 400°F.

(continued)

Trim the stalks off the fennel bulbs and remove the outer layer of the bulb, reserving it and the stalks for stock and a few fronds for garnish. Cut the bulb crosswise into ¼- to ½-inch-thick slices. Spread the fennel over a large baking sheet. Drizzle each with 2 tablespoons olive oil, season with salt (about 1 teaspoon), and toss to coat. Spread the fennel into an even layer and roast until golden at the edges but not yet tender, about 15 minutes. Remove from the oven and set aside.

When the beans are ready, set a large Dutch oven over medium heat, add 2 tablespoons olive oil, and give it a minute to heat up. Add the garlic and leeks and cook, stirring occasionally, until the leeks are tender and translucent, about 10 minutes. Stir in the sun-dried tomatoes, thyme, anchovies, and roasted fennel. Add the Pernod and let it bubble for a minute or so, scraping all the tasty browned bits off the bottom of the pan with a wooden spoon.

Add the beans, stock, Calabrian chile, and 2 teaspoons salt and bring to a simmer over medium-high heat. Adjust the heat to maintain a moderate simmer and cook until the liquid reduces to a saucy, buttery consistency and the beans are creamy but not falling apart, 5 to 10 minutes. If the liquid is too thick before the beans are done, add a generous splash of the reserved bean cooking liquid.

Turn off the heat. Stir in the crème fraîche, butter, piment d'Espelette, parsley, lemon zest, lemon juice, and 1 teaspoon salt. Season to taste with pepper and more salt and lemon juice.

Serve in the pot, garnished with the reserved fennel fronds and a nice drizzle of olive oil.

Fava Beans in Bacon Broth with Hearts of Palm and Caramelized Shallots

This is a special dish born from a strange moment. It was the spring of 2020. Restaurants and stores were empty, but my garden was flourishing. To keep busy and keep fear at bay, I got to picking the fava pods that had been growing like a weed. I didn't want them to go to waste. My project for the day was figuring out a way to get Hudson to eat them.

I combed my fridge and cupboards, grabbing various vegetables and a slab of bacon, both a few days from spoiled, and threw them in a pot with water to simmer. Meanwhile, I shelled, blanched, and peeled those favas. The bacony broth; those grassy, sweet beans; and some crisp, juicy hearts of palm I excavated from a dusty can—it was so good that I now make it on purpose whenever spring rolls around.

SERVES 4

Kosher salt
4 pounds fresh fava bean pods, shelled
3 thick slices bacon, cut crosswise into roughly ¼-inch-wide pieces
A splash of extra-virgin olive oil
2 cups thinly sliced shallots (about 4 large)
½ teaspoon sugar
8 ounces canned or jarred hearts of palm, drained, rinsed, and sliced into ½-inch pieces (about 1½ cups)
2 cups Bacon Broth (recipe follows), hot
Thinly sliced fresh chives, for garnish

Bring a medium pot of water to a boil. While you wait, fill a medium bowl with lots of ice and water (this will be your shocking station).

When the water comes to a boil, salt it heavily so it tastes like the sea. Add the favas and boil until tender, 1 to 2 minutes. To check for doneness, drop one bean into the ice bath, peel off the skin, and taste it: It should be tender (no longer gritty) but retain a slight bite. When they're ready, scoop them out with a strainer and add them to the ice bath. Let cool, then drain, peel off and discard their outer skins, and set aside.

Set a large skillet over medium-low heat, add the bacon and a splash of oil, and cook, stirring occasionally, until crisp, 8 to 10 minutes. Transfer the bacon to a small bowl. Pour off about half the bacon fat (reserving it for another purpose), leaving the rest in the skillet, and set aside.

Add the shallots and a good sprinkle of salt to the skillet. Cook over medium heat, stirring and scraping the pan occasionally, until the shallots turn golden brown, 8 to 10 minutes. Add the sugar and cook, stirring frequently, until the shallots are deep golden brown, about 10 minutes, adding a splash of water and scraping the skillet if they threaten to burn. Remove the pan from the heat.

Divide the favas and hearts of palm evenly among four shallow bowls and top with the caramelized shallots. Ladle about ½ cup of the bacon broth into each bowl, garnish with the bacon and chives, and serve.

(continued)

Bacon Broth

MAKES 4 CUPS

1 tablespoon extra-virgin olive oil
1 pound slab bacon, cut into 1 by 1-inch pieces
2 celery stalks, coarsely chopped
1 large carrot, coarsely chopped
1 large leek, white and pale green parts only, halved lengthwise, cleaned, and coarsely chopped
1 large yellow onion, coarsely chopped
1 bay leaf
1 (2-inch) piece fresh ginger, peeled and chopped
3 star anise pods
6 garlic cloves, peeled
6 thyme sprigs
1 tablespoon soy sauce
Kosher salt and freshly ground black pepper

Set a large stockpot over medium heat and add the olive oil. When the oil is hot, add the bacon, celery, carrot, leek, and onion and cook, stirring occasionally, until the carrot starts to soften and the bacon starts to brown at the edges, about 15 minutes.

Add the bay leaf, ginger, star anise, garlic, thyme, and 8 cups water. Raise the heat to high and bring to a simmer, then reduce the heat to maintain a gentle simmer and cook until the bacon is so tender, it starts to fall apart and the broth has a rich, smoky bacon flavor, 1 to 1½ hours.

Strain the broth into a large bowl and discard the solids. Let it cool completely, then cover and refrigerate overnight (this makes it easy to remove the fat).

The next day, scrape off the solid layer of fat from the surface of the broth. (Reserve it for another purpose, like roasting vegetables, because it's delicious.) Simmer the broth in a medium saucepan for 10 minutes or so, then add the soy sauce and have a taste. Season to taste with salt (start with 1 teaspoon) and pepper (about ¼ teaspoon).

Serve the broth hot, or let cool, then store in airtight containers in the fridge for up to 5 days or in the freezer for up to 3 months.

Haricot Vert and Soba Salad with Avocado, Radish, and Hibiscus Ponzu

I'm a big fan of soba salads that are all about the noodles. But I also like to flip the script and make a soba salad that's all about the veg. Haricots verts, slim green beans with a lovely tender crunch, are the star of this dish, with crisp radishes and creamy pieces of avocado playing backup. The dressing makes a real splash: I tweak the classic ponzu, the Japanese condiment made from citrus and soy sauce, by opting for fragrant Meyer lemon rather than the more typical yuzu and adding highly nontraditional dried hibiscus flowers, which contribute another dimension of acidity as well as a striking fuchsia color.

SERVES 4 TO 6

For the ponzu

⅓ cup Meyer lemon juice (from about 2 lemons)
⅓ cup white soy sauce (see Note)
¼ cup crumbled dried hibiscus flowers
2 tablespoons mirin
2 big pinches katsuobushi (bonito flakes)
1 tablespoon sugar
1 large piece kombu (about 4 by 8 inches), coarsely crumbled

For the salad

Kosher salt
¾ pound haricots verts
8 ounces buckwheat soba noodles
2 teaspoons extra-virgin olive oil
2 teaspoons toasted sesame oil
¼ cup dried ogo or hijiki seaweed, rehydrated according to the package instructions
3 scallions, thinly sliced on an angle
1 small watermelon radish, sliced into thin matchsticks (about ½ cup)
1 ripe but firm Hass avocado, cubed
Handful of cilantro, coarsely chopped
1 tablespoon toasted sesame seeds

Make the ponzu

Combine the ponzu ingredients in a container, add ¼ cup water, and stir well. Cover and refrigerate for at least 4 hours or up to 12 hours. Pour the ponzu through a fine-mesh strainer into a bowl, discarding the solids. Cover and refrigerate until chilled or for up to 5 days.

Make the salad

Bring a medium pot of water to a boil and add a handful of salt. Fill a large bowl with ice and water. Add the haricots verts to the boiling water and cook for 1 minute, or until they're no longer raw but still nice and snappy. Use a strainer to transfer them to the ice water (keep the pot at a boil). Let them cool completely, then drain well.

Add the soba noodles to the boiling water and cook, stirring occasionally, until tender but not mushy, 4 to 5 minutes. Drain, run them under cold water to rinse off the starch and cool the noodles, then drain again really well and transfer to a large bowl.

Add the olive oil, sesame oil, and seaweed to the noodles and toss to combine.

Divide the noodles among shallow bowls and garnish with the scallions, radish, avocado, cilantro, and haricots verts. Sprinkle on the sesame seeds and pour in the ponzu so it pools at the bottom. Serve and have everyone toss well before they dig in.

Note: You can totally sub the darker regular soy sauce for the white soy sauce I call for here, though you'll be sacrificing the ponzu's bright color.

Stewed Chickpeas with Harissa, Date, and Chorizo

These rich, stewy chickpeas make a head-turning one-pot dinner. They're full of dark thrills—the dried-chile heat and spice of harissa, caramel-sweet dates, and chorizo, which pervades the dish with dusky, porky goodness. The juice of blood oranges adds such a lovely complexity to the stew, and juicy segments add brightness to the simple peppery salad I serve on top.

SERVES 4 TO 6

For the stew

1 tablespoon extra-virgin olive oil
6 ounces fresh Mexican chorizo, casing removed
1 cup thinly sliced red onion
1½ tablespoons harissa
1½ tablespoons tomato paste
3 garlic cloves, sliced
Zest of 2 blood oranges
Juice of 3 blood oranges
1½ tablespoons honey
3 cups drained cooked or rinsed canned chickpeas
1½ cups unsalted chicken stock
3 tablespoons unsalted butter
8 Medjool dates, pitted and quartered lengthwise
Kosher salt

For serving

3 blood oranges
3 large handfuls of arugula (I like the wild stuff here)
½ cup thinly sliced red onion
1 generous tablespoon extra-virgin olive oil
Flaky sea salt, like Maldon

Make the stew

Set a large skillet over medium-high heat, add the olive oil, and heat until it shimmers. Add the chorizo and cook, breaking it up with a spoon as you go, until it's cooked through, 3 to 5 minutes. Add the onion and cook, stirring occasionally, until it has softened a bit, 3 to 5 minutes.

Add the harissa, tomato paste, and garlic and cook, stirring constantly, until the tomato paste and harissa darken a bit and begin to dry out, 1 to 2 minutes. Add the blood orange zest, blood orange juice, and honey and stir, scraping up all the tasty browned bits from the bottom of the pan with a wooden spoon. Add the chickpeas and stock, let it come to a strong simmer, and cook, stirring occasionally, until the liquid reduces by about half and becomes thick and saucy, 5 to 7 minutes. Stir in the butter and dates and remove from the heat. Season to taste with salt (up to 2 teaspoons, depending on how salty the chorizo is) and keep warm.

Just before serving, cut the ends off the blood oranges to reveal the flesh, then carve off the peel and pith. Holding one orange over a medium bowl, cut the segments from the membranes, letting them fall into the bowl. When you're done, squeeze in the juice from the membranes. Repeat with the remaining oranges.

Add the arugula and thinly sliced onion to the bowl with the blood orange segments and juice. Drizzle with the olive oil, sprinkle with flaky salt, and toss gently to coat.

Spoon the stewed chickpeas into a large, shallow serving dish, top with the salad, and serve.

BONUS COCKTAIL

Blood Orange Negroni

MAKES 1

1½ ounces (3 tablespoons) fresh blood orange juice
1 ounce (2 tablespoons) Lillet Blanc
1 ounce (2 tablespoons) Campari
1 ounce (2 tablespoons) gin
1 thin slice blood orange, for garnish (optional)
Ice cubes

Combine the orange juice, Lillet, Campari, and gin in an ice-filled cocktail shaker and shake well. Strain into an ice-filled rocks glass (or strain into a coupe and serve up). Garnish with the blood orange slice, if desired.

Smashed-Pea Fritters with Garlic Yogurt (and, Maybe, Caviar)

Like so many chefs, I'm a big fan of frozen peas, which are consistently sweet and less starchy than their fresh counterparts. I wouldn't serve them in a salad as I'd do with blanched in-season pods (unless that salad has mayo-dressed potatoes), but I will blend them to make soup, toss them in fried rice, and maybe best of all, make these fritters, which take advantage of their best attributes. A little dill and lemon zest, along with the zippy garlic-yogurt sauce, brings a lightness to these crisp-edged beauties. Caviar is entirely unnecessary but also very much welcome.

MAKES 8 OR 9 FRITTERS

For the yogurt sauce

20 garlic cloves, peeled
½ cup plain full-fat Greek yogurt
Finely grated zest of 1 lemon
2 tablespoons lemon juice, plus more if needed
1 tablespoon extra-virgin olive oil
1 teaspoon kosher salt, plus more if needed
Big pinch of chopped fresh dill

For the fritters

2 garlic cloves, grated on a Microplane
2 large eggs
Kosher salt and freshly ground black pepper
2 cups frozen peas, thawed
Finely grated zest of 1 lemon
Big pinch of chopped fresh dill, plus some sprigs for garnish
1 teaspoon ground turmeric
1 medium leek, white and pale green parts only, halved lengthwise, cleaned, and thinly sliced
⅓ cup all-purpose flour
1 tablespoon cornstarch
½ teaspoon baking powder
½ cup neutral oil, like canola
Flaky sea salt, like Maldon
Caviar, any kind, as much as you can handle (optional)

Make the yogurt sauce

Bring about 4 inches of water to a gentle boil in a medium saucepan. Add the garlic and cook just until it's smooshable soft, about 20 minutes. Drain the garlic and let cool completely. (If you're in a rush, dunk the cloves in ice water to speed things along, then drain again.)

Put the garlic in a medium bowl and mash and stir until smooth. Add the yogurt, lemon zest, lemon juice, olive oil, salt, and dill and mix well. Season to taste with more salt and lemon juice. Refrigerate until chilled.

The yogurt sauce keeps in an airtight container in the fridge for up to 1 day.

(continued)

Make the fritters

Preheat the oven to 200°F.

Put the garlic, eggs, 2 teaspoons salt, ½ teaspoon pepper, and 1 cup of the peas in a food processor and puree until smooth. Transfer to a medium bowl, add the lemon zest, dill, turmeric, and leeks, and stir to combine.

In a small bowl, stir together the flour, cornstarch, and baking powder. Add the flour mixture to the vegetable mixture and mix well just until there are no more spots of the flour. Stir in the remaining 1 cup peas.

Line a large baking sheet with paper towels. Set a 14-inch cast-iron skillet over medium heat, add the neutral oil, and heat until it shimmers. Working in batches so you don't crowd the pan, spoon 4 dollops of batter (about ¼ cup each) into the pan, leaving a little space between each one. Cook until golden brown and crisp on the first side, 2 to 3 minutes. Flip the fritters, give them each a light press to flatten them slightly, and cook until golden brown and crisp on the second side, 2 to 3 minutes more. Transfer the fritters to the prepared baking sheet in a single layer, sprinkle with flaky salt, and pop them in the oven to keep warm. Repeat with the remaining batter.

Serve the fritters on a platter, garnished with dill sprigs, yogurt sauce, and maybe caviar.

Triple Threat Pea Salad with Meyer Lemon Dressing and Feta

Make this salad when and only when fresh peas flood the farmers' market. That's when they deserve to be center stage in all their glory. I like to use them in three varieties—raw sugar snaps with their candy-sweetness and crisp edible pods; English peas blanched so they're tender with a little pop; and pea greens for their delicate grassy flavor. The dressing and tangy feta provides plenty of brightness to keep the spring sweetness in check, but since you're already trawling the market for peas, it's worth seeking out sorrel, too, for the refreshing sour note it brings.

SERVES 4

For the dressing

3 tablespoons extra-virgin olive oil
1 tablespoon honey
1 tablespoon champagne vinegar or white wine vinegar
1 teaspoon Dijon mustard
1 teaspoon kosher salt
½ teaspoon red chile flakes
¼ teaspoon freshly ground black pepper
1 garlic clove, grated on a Microplane
1 medium shallot, minced
Zest of 1 Meyer lemon
¼ cup Meyer lemon juice

For the salad

1½ cups shelled fresh English peas (from 1½ to 2 pounds pods)
Kosher salt
¼ cup baby sorrel (optional)
Small handful of mint leaves, sliced at the last minute
Small handful of dill
⅓ cup crumbled feta cheese
⅓ cup roasted unsalted hazelnuts, coarsely chopped
2 handfuls of pea tendrils, any thick stems removed
1 pound sugar snap peas, thinly sliced on an angle
Flaky sea salt, like Maldon
Freshly ground black pepper

Make the dressing

Whisk together all the dressing ingredients in a large bowl.

Make the salad

Bring a medium saucepan of water to a boil and generously salt it. Fill a large bowl with ice and water. Add the peas to the boiling water and cook until no longer starchy, 1½ to 2 minutes. Drain the peas and plunge them into the ice water. Let cool, then drain them really well.

Add the peas, sorrel (if using), mint, dill, half of the feta, half of the hazelnuts, the pea tendrils, and sugar snap peas to the bowl with the dressing and gently toss to coat. Transfer the salad to a serving platter and sprinkle on the remaining feta and hazelnuts along with some flaky salt and a generous amount of pepper and serve.

TOMATOES

Juicy Gems

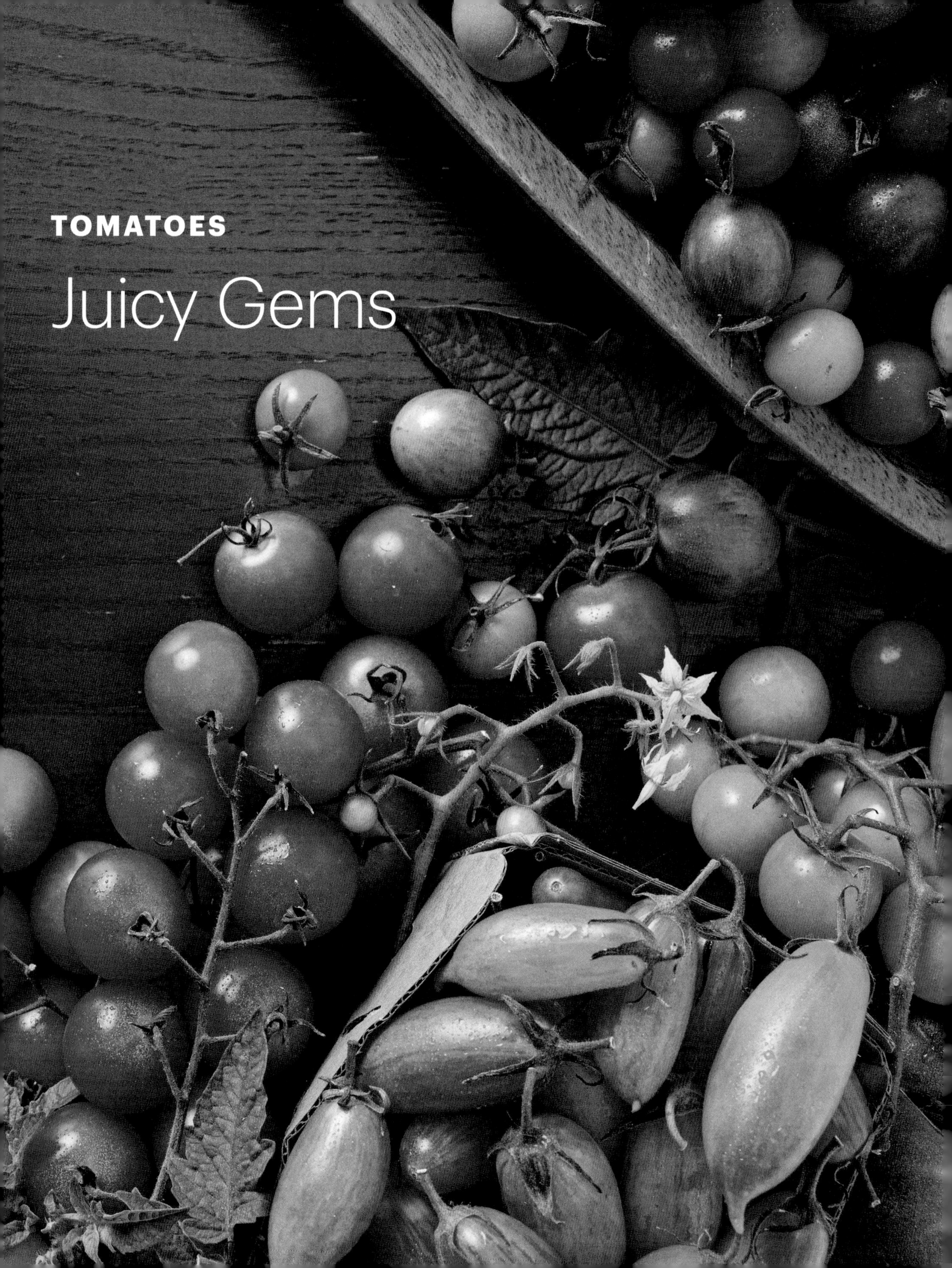

Anchovy and Butter-Roasted Sungold Tomatoes with Wheat Berries and Radishes

Every summer I face the happy problem of figuring out how to use the bounty of Sungolds that grow like mad in my garden. This preparation is one of my faves: You roast the vivid orange, sweet-tart orbs with anchovies, butter, vinegar, and thyme until they burst. Then into all those juices, you nestle sweet onions, juicy cooked radishes (a revelation if you have only tried them raw), and wheat berries, which soak up the fun and hearty up the dish to take it from the side to the center of the table.

SERVES 4

1 pound peeled cipollini onions or small shallots, halved crosswise
2 bunches small round radishes, cut about the same size as the onions
Extra-virgin olive oil
Kosher salt and freshly ground black pepper
2 pounds cherry tomatoes (I love Sungolds here)
1 stick (½ cup) unsalted butter
¼ cup sherry vinegar
10 oil-packed anchovy fillets, drained
8 thyme sprigs
6 garlic cloves, minced
2 teaspoons piment d'Espelette, plus more for serving
2 cups cooked wheat berries

Preheat the oven to 400°F.

Put the onions and radishes (save the greens for later) in a 9 by 13-inch baking dish, drizzle with 2 tablespoons olive oil, season with 2 teaspoons salt and pepper to taste, and toss to coat. Roast, stirring once, until light golden brown and tender with a slight bite, 12 to 15 minutes. Transfer the onions and radishes to a plate and set aside. Keep the oven on.

In the same baking dish, combine the tomatoes, butter, vinegar, anchovies, thyme, garlic, piment d'Espelette, ¼ cup olive oil, 2 teaspoons salt, and pepper to taste and toss well. Roast, rotating the baking dish occasionally, until the tomatoes begin to burst, 8 to 10 minutes.

Nestle the onions, radishes, and wheat berries into the tomato mixture, getting them into those juices without stirring and potentially smashing the tomatoes. Return the baking dish to the oven for 5 minutes more, just so the wheat berries have the chance to soak up some of those buttery tomato juices.

Remove the baking dish from the oven, sprinkle on a little more piment d'Espelette, and serve.

Note: If the radish greens are pretty and unblemished, give them a rinse and reserve them. Then, right after you remove the baking dish from the oven, toss them in so they wilt.

Cherry Tomato–Stone Fruit Salad with Pickled Shallots and Black Lentil Dressing

I love treating tomatoes like the fruits they are. Pairing their juicy brightness and sweetness with nectarines, plums, and cherries—juicy, bright, and sweet themselves and at their peak at the same time tomatoes are—it's one of many great examples of the grow-together-go-together principle of cooking. Besides finding top-notch produce, all you've got to do is make a simple dressing that features a little extra sweetness to really showcase those fruits and black lentils to add some surprising texture.

SERVES 4

For the dressing

¼ cup red wine vinegar
2 tablespoons sugar
2 teaspoons kosher salt
3 small shallots: 2 thinly sliced into rings, 1 minced
1 teaspoon whole-grain mustard
1 teaspoon Dijon mustard
3 tablespoons extra-virgin olive oil
⅓ cup cooked beluga or Puy lentils
Freshly ground black pepper

For the salad

1 pound mixed stone fruit, pitted, cut into bite-size pieces, and chilled for 30 minutes or so
8 ounces heirloom cherry tomatoes (a mix of colors is nice), halved and chilled for 30 minutes or so
Handful of basil leaves, thinly sliced at the last minute
¼ cup chopped (1-inch) fresh chives
Flaky sea salt, like Maldon
Freshly ground black pepper

Make the dressing

Whisk together the vinegar, sugar, and 1 teaspoon of the salt in a small bowl. Add the sliced shallots, toss to coat, and let them pickle slightly, at least 15 minutes.

Use a slotted spoon to scoop the shallots into a small bowl and set aside. Add the minced shallot and mustards to the pickling liquid, then, while whisking constantly, drizzle in the olive oil. Stir in the lentils, the remaining 1 teaspoon salt, and pepper to taste.

Make the salad

When you're ready to serve, combine the stone fruit, tomatoes, herbs, pickled shallots, and about half the dressing in a large bowl and toss gently but well. Transfer to a serving plate and spoon on the remaining dressing. Add a sprinkle of flaky salt and pepper to taste, then serve.

Panzanella with Marinated Tomatoes, Charred Onion, and Pomegranate

In many ways this is a classic panzanella—gorgeous summer tomatoes marinated to accentuate their best qualities, fresh herbs, and olive oil–toasted bread to soak up all those yummy juices. Yet I also take the Tuscan salad in an unexpected direction: Because juicy end of season tomatoes often coincide with pomegranate season—I remember picking pomegranates from the tree in my yard while it was still hot out—I look to their seeds to add pops of flavor and texture. A little pomegranate molasses in the marinade underscores their dark, sultry tartness.

SERVES 4

For the bread

½ loaf good crusty bread, torn into ½-inch pieces (about 4 cups)

3 tablespoons Garlic Confit oil (see page 119) or extra-virgin olive oil

1½ teaspoons kosher salt

For the tomatoes

⅓ cup extra-virgin olive oil

¼ cup apple cider vinegar

2 tablespoons honey

2 tablespoons pomegranate molasses

2 teaspoons Dijon mustard

1 teaspoon kosher salt

1 teaspoon freshly ground black pepper

¼ teaspoon red chile flakes

1 small shallot, minced

1½ pounds assorted summer heirloom tomatoes, cut into bite-size pieces

For the salad

1 tablespoon neutral oil, like canola

1 medium red onion, cut into 1-inch wedges through the root nub (so they stay intact)

Kosher salt and freshly ground black pepper

8 ounces fresh mozzarella cheese, cut about the same size as the tomatoes

½ cup pomegranate seeds

Handful of mixed chopped fresh herbs (like basil, parsley, oregano, and scallions)

Prep the bread

Preheat the oven to 350°F.

Combine the bread, confit oil, and salt in a medium bowl and toss to coat. Spread the bread over a large baking sheet and bake, stirring once, until almost crunchy all the way through (a little chew in the center is nice), 10 to 12 minutes.

Prep the tomatoes

Whisk together the olive oil, vinegar, honey, molasses, mustard, salt, pepper, chile flakes, and shallot in a large bowl. Add the tomatoes, toss gently to coat, and set aside to marinate, gently stirring once or twice, for 10 to 20 minutes, so they have a chance to absorb some flavor.

Make the salad

While the tomatoes marinate, set a medium pan over medium-high heat, add the oil, and heat until it shimmers. Add the onion wedges and cook, flipping them once, until deeply charred on both sides, about 2 minutes per side. Lightly season both sides of the onions with salt and pepper, transfer them to a cutting board, and let them cool slightly. Trim off the root nubs and separate into pieces.

When you're ready to serve, add the toasted bread, charred onions, mozzarella, pomegranate seeds, and herbs to the bowl with the tomatoes and toss gently but well. Season to taste with salt and pepper and serve on a platter.

Slow-Cooked Tomato Toasts with Whipped Ricotta, Saffron, and Honey

Whipped ricotta on toast is really good. Topped with these sweet roasted tomatoes, infused with saffron, fennel, and thyme, it's next-level. I especially love how the orange zest in the ricotta plays with the saffron, and how the tomatoes hold their shape but still get jammy and concentrated in flavor. A drizzle of honey plays up the fruitiness of the tomatoes and ties all the elements together.

SERVES 4

For the tomatoes

2 teaspoons saffron threads
2 (12-ounce) packages Campari or cherry tomatoes on the vine
3 tablespoons extra-virgin olive oil
2 teaspoons fennel seeds, toasted and very coarsely ground
2 teaspoons chopped fresh thyme leaves
½ teaspoon red chile flakes
3 garlic cloves, thinly sliced
1 teaspoon kosher salt
¼ teaspoon freshly ground black pepper

For the ricotta

1 cup whole-milk ricotta cheese
⅓ cup heavy cream
Finely grated zest of ½ navel orange
1 teaspoon kosher salt, plus more as needed
¼ teaspoon freshly ground black pepper

For serving

4 (½-inch-thick) slices crusty bread
Extra-virgin olive oil
Kosher salt and freshly ground black pepper
2 tablespoons or so honey, for drizzling

Make the tomatoes

Preheat the oven to 350°F.

Crumble the saffron threads in a small bowl, add 1 tablespoon very hot tap water, and let steep, stirring occasionally, for 20 minutes.

Combine the tomatoes, olive oil, fennel seeds, thyme, chile flakes, garlic, salt, pepper, and the saffron mixture in a shallow 9-inch square baking dish and toss well. Roast, spooning the pan juices over the tomatoes once or twice along the way, until the tomatoes begin to burst (but before they fall off the vines), 12 to 15 minutes. Remove from the oven and let cool to room temperature.

Whip the ricotta and serve

Meanwhile, combine the ricotta, cream, orange zest, salt, and pepper in the bowl of a stand mixer fitted with the whisk attachment (or in a mini food processor) and beat on medium speed (or pulse) to combine well. Beat on high (or process), stopping once to scrape down the sides, until light and fluffy, 2 to 3 minutes more. Season to taste with more salt and set aside.

Set a grill pan or large heavy-bottomed skillet over medium-high heat. Generously drizzle both sides of the bread with olive oil and season lightly with salt and pepper. Grill each slice of bread, turning once, until lightly charred on both sides, about 30 seconds per side. Let the bread cool to room temperature.

Generously slather each piece of grilled bread with whipped ricotta, drizzle with honey, and season with pepper. Top with the tomatoes just before serving.

Summer Heirloom Salad with Sweet Onion and Crab–Yuzu Kosho Dressing

Perfect tomatoes don't need much—a drizzle of good olive oil, a sprinkle of flaky salt. But when I'm having friends over and want to do something a little special, I deck out those gorgeous heirlooms with chunks of sweet crab. Typically the focus of a dish, the crab here is a garnish, lending its salinity and luxury to summer's finest. Tying it all together is a punchy dressing bright with the irreplaceable flavor of yuzu and fiery from fresh chile and yuzu kosho.

SERVES 4

For the crab dressing

¼ cup unseasoned rice vinegar
2 tablespoons honey
1½ tablespoons yuzu juice (bottled is just fine here)
1 teaspoon Dijon mustard
1 teaspoon whole-grain mustard
1½ teaspoons green or red yuzu kosho
1 teaspoon kosher salt
¼ teaspoon freshly ground black pepper
2 garlic cloves, grated on a Microplane
½ to 1 serrano chile, thinly sliced
3 tablespoons extra-virgin olive oil
2 teaspoons toasted sesame oil
8 ounces Dungeness crabmeat or lump crabmeat, picked over for any shell fragments
1 tablespoon thinly sliced fresh chives

For the salad

1½ pounds assorted heirloom tomatoes, cored and cut into ½-inch-thick slices
½ cup very thinly sliced (a mandoline helps) sweet onion, like Vidalia or Maui
Flaky sea salt, like Maldon

Make the dressing

Whisk together the vinegar, honey, yuzu juice, both mustards, the yuzu kosho, salt, pepper, garlic, and chile in a medium bowl. While whisking constantly, slowly stream in the olive oil and then the sesame oil. Just before serving, gently fold the crab and chives into the dressing.

Make the salad

Arrange the tomatoes and shaved onions on a serving platter and sprinkle evenly with flaky salt. Spoon on the crab dressing and serve.

Note: Yuzu kosho is a mixture of fermented yuzu rind and chile. It's so delightfully intense that just one of the tiny jars it's sold in will provide months' worth of fun.

Tomato-Stewed Fregola with Baked Eggs and Guanciale

This might present like a dish of baked eggs, but it eats like baked pasta. Fregola, after all, is a rustic Sardinian pasta that's dried in the sun and toasted to make irregular pearls that range from golden to brown—imperfection at its finest. Each bite gives you that orzo feeling—the delight of eating dozens of little noodles at once—with rich jammy stewed tomatoes imbued with guanciale's irresistible porkiness.

After the fregola soaks up all that goodness, you spoon on a dead-simple fresh tomato salad for brightness and another dimension of flavor and acidity. The eggs are more condiment than everyone-gets-one. When you're ready to serve, break them up so the runny yolks enrich the sauce.

SERVES 4

For the baked eggs

Extra-virgin olive oil
4 ounces guanciale or pancetta, diced
1 small yellow onion, finely diced
3 garlic cloves, thinly sliced
1 tablespoon tomato paste
2 teaspoons crushed Calabrian chile, or more to taste
2½ cups unsalted chicken stock or water
1 (15-ounce) can whole peeled tomatoes (preferably real San Marzanos), crushed
1½ cups cherry tomatoes, halved
2 teaspoons sugar
Kosher salt
1 teaspoon dried oregano
1 cup fregola or Israeli couscous
4 large eggs
¼ teaspoon freshly ground black pepper

For the tomato salad

1 tablespoon minced shallot
2 tablespoons sherry vinegar
3 tablespoons extra-virgin olive oil
½ cup cherry tomatoes, halved
Handful of basil leaves, thinly sliced at the last minute
Handful of flat-leaf parsley, coarsely chopped
Kosher salt and freshly ground black pepper

Make the baked eggs

Preheat the oven to 400°F.

Set a 12-inch heavy skillet over medium heat, add a splash of olive oil and the guanciale, and cook, stirring occasionally, until the guanciale begins to brown and crisp, about 5 minutes. Stir in the onion and garlic and cook until the onion softens and the garlic is fragrant, 3 to 4 minutes.

Add the tomato paste and cook, stirring constantly, until it darkens a bit and begins to dry out, 1 to 2 minutes. Stir in the Calabrian chile. Add the stock, canned tomatoes, cherry tomatoes, sugar, 2 teaspoons salt, and the oregano, stir well, and let it come to a simmer. Stir in the fregola, cover, and cook, stirring once, until the fregola is tender but still retains a slight bite, about 20 minutes.

Use a spoon to make 4 divots in the fregola mixture, leaving a little space between each one. One at a time, carefully crack the eggs into a ramekin (so you can discard any shell pieces), then tuck one egg into each divot in the fregola. Give each egg a light sprinkle of salt and pepper.

Transfer the pan to the oven and bake, uncovered, rotating the skillet once halfway through, until the egg whites are just set (they'll continue to cook slightly when you remove them from the oven) but the yolks are still runny, about 10 minutes.

Make the tomato salad

Meanwhile, combine the shallot and vinegar in a medium bowl and set aside to marinate for at least 5 minutes to tame the shallot's raw bite. Add the olive oil, cherry tomatoes, herbs, and salt and pepper to taste and toss gently but well.

When the eggs are done, spoon on the tomato salad and serve.

CORN

Sweet All Year Long

Corn and Salt Cod Chowder

This soup has all the pleasures of a corn chowder, that summer sweetness balanced by a bit of cream. Yet I look to clam juice (a staple in my pantry) to evoke a different sort of chowder and to salt cod (my obsession) to add a layer of unexpected salty goodness. If you've never used salt cod, you've got to try it: Deboned and sold in little wooden boxes, it keeps more or less forever (that salt works wonders). After a brief soak, it contributes a backbone of umami to soups and stews that your guests might not be able to place but one they'll absolutely love.

SERVES 4 TO 6

1 tablespoon extra-virgin olive oil
1 large carrot, diced into ¼-inch pieces
1 celery stalk, diced into ¼-inch pieces
1 medium yellow onion, diced into ¼-inch pieces
4 garlic cloves, minced
4 ounces salt cod, soaked overnight in water, drained, rinsed, and diced (about 1 cup)
1½ tablespoons kosher salt
½ teaspoon red chile flakes
1 bay leaf
4 large ears corn, shucked
1 cup clam juice
1 large russet potato, peeled and diced into ½-inch pieces
1 cup heavy cream
Finely grated zest and juice of 1 lemon, or more to taste
2 tablespoons thinly sliced fresh chives

Heat the olive oil in a large heavy-bottomed pot or Dutch oven over medium heat until it shimmers. Add the carrot, celery, onion, garlic, salt cod, ½ tablespoon of the salt, the chile flakes, and bay leaf. Cook, stirring occasionally, until the vegetables soften a bit (but don't let them brown), 10 to 15 minutes.

Meanwhile, working over a bowl, cut the kernels off the corncobs, then use the back of the knife to scrape the cobs to get anything you left behind. Reserve the cobs. Transfer half the corn mixture to a blender, add 4 cups water, and blend until smooth.

When the vegetables have softened, add the clam juice, blended corn mixture, and scraped corncobs. Bring to a simmer, then cook, stirring occasionally, for 30 minutes. Remove and discard the corncobs, then add the remaining whole corn kernels and the potatoes. Cook, stirring occasionally, until the potatoes are soft but not falling apart, about 15 minutes.

Stir in the cream, lemon zest, lemon juice, and the remaining 1 tablespoon salt. Season to taste with more salt and lemon juice. Serve garnished with the chives.

Arepas with Caramelized Onion, Mozzarella, Ham, and Salsa Macha

When you compete on food TV, you're often presented with ingredients you're entirely unfamiliar with, and sometimes, it shows. Other times, you get lucky and inspired. On *Bobby's Triple Threat*, I was tasked with cooking with yuca (also known as cassava) and I attempted a variation on arepas, the crisp-edged savory corn cakes beloved in Venezuela and Colombia. They were so tasty that I thought, *I should totally learn to make these in real life.*

So I got in the habit at home, digging into cookbooks and YouTube videos by true arepa buffs. I look to a simple dough from the more traditional corn flour, and stuff arepas with all sorts of fun. My favorite filling so far is fresh corn along with gooey cheese, caramelized onions, and my dad's favorite, Black Forest ham. On top, I like to drizzle on an oily, smoky salsa from Veracruz, Mexico, that's completely unrelated but also completely delicious.

MAKES 8

For the filling

1 tablespoon unsalted butter
2 teaspoons extra-virgin olive oil
1 small yellow onion, sliced
1 teaspoon light brown sugar
1 teaspoon kosher salt, plus more as needed
½ teaspoon freshly ground black pepper, plus more as needed
Kernels from 1 large ear corn
2 ounces thinly sliced Black Forest ham, cut into strips (about ½ cup)
4 ounces fresh mozzarella cheese, cut into smallish pieces (about ½ cup)

For the arepas

1 heaping teaspoon kosher salt
2 cups masarepa (I like the white variety, but yellow will also work), plus more as needed
¼ cup neutral oil, like canola

For serving

Salsa Macha (recipe follows)
Chopped fresh cilantro
Lime wedges

Prep the filling

Combine the butter and olive oil in a medium pan over medium-high heat. When the butter melts and froths, add the onion and brown sugar. Reduce the heat to medium and cook, stirring frequently, until the onion turns caramel brown and fully soft but not jammy, 15 to 20 minutes. Season with salt and pepper.

Stir in the corn and cook, stirring occasionally, just until the corn is tender, about 2 minutes. Remove from the heat, stir in the ham, and let cool completely. Stir in the mozzarella and season to taste with more salt and pepper.

(continued)

Make the arepas

Preheat the oven to 400°F.

Combine 2 cups warm water and the salt in a large bowl, give it a quick stir, then add the masarepa. Mix and knead the mixture with your hands until it comes together into a dough. It should be moist but not sticky—if it's sticky, add a little more masarepa; if it's dry, add a little more water. Cover with a damp paper towel and let the dough rest for 5 to 10 minutes.

Cut the dough into 16 equal pieces. Work with two pieces at a time, keeping the rest covered with the towel. Roll each piece into a ball, then press to flatten it into a roughly ½-inch-thick disc.

Form one disc into a shallow bowl, pressing down in the middle and pinching the edges to make a bowl shape, and add a heaping tablespoon of the filling. Lay the second disc on top and pinch the edges together to seal, then pat and shape the arepa to look like a little hockey puck. Set the filled arepa aside, covered with damp paper towels, and repeat with the rest of the dough and filling.

Heat the oil in a large cast-iron or nonstick skillet over medium heat until it shimmers. Working in batches to avoid crowding, add the arepas and cook, flipping once, until golden brown on both sides, 4 to 5 minutes per side. Transfer to a large baking sheet and repeat to cook the remaining arepas.

Transfer the baking sheet to the oven and bake the arepas for 5 minutes, or until the center is hot and gooey. Serve hot, topped with salsa macha and cilantro and with lime wedges on the side.

Salsa Macha

MAKES ABOUT 1½ CUPS

1 cup avocado oil or other neutral oil
2 ancho chiles, stemmed, slit open, and seeded
2 guajillo chiles, stemmed, slit open, and seeded
4 chiles de árbol, stemmed
10 garlic cloves, coarsely chopped
1 medium shallot, coarsely chopped
⅓ cup unsalted roasted peanuts
1 tablespoon plus 1 teaspoon apple cider vinegar
2½ teaspoons kosher salt
1 teaspoon honey
Finely grated zest and juice of 1 lime

Heat the avocado oil in a medium saucepan over medium heat just until it bubbles lightly when you dunk the edge of a chile into the oil. Add all the chiles and fry, stirring occasionally, until the bubbling subsides and they've turned a shade or two darker, about 2 minutes. Use a slotted spoon to transfer the chiles to a food processor.

Add the garlic and shallot to the oil and fry until light golden, 1 to 2 minutes. Remove the pan from the heat and transfer the garlic and shallot to the food processor with a slotted spoon. Let the oil in the skillet cool to warm.

Add the peanuts and warm oil to the food processor and pulse to a very coarse puree. Add the vinegar, salt, honey, lime zest, and lime juice and pulse once or twice more just to combine.

The salsa is great now but even better the next day, and will keep in an airtight container in the fridge for up to 1 week.

Cheddar Cornbread with Date Butter

Proper cornbread, I'm told by those who have cooked cornbread all their lives, doesn't contain sugar. The story goes that back in the day, Southern cooks used a sweeter corn for milling, so the cornmeal of old didn't require any top-ups. But I'll admit it—I like mine plenty sweet, with a good dose of sugar, canned creamed corn, and even fresh kernels in the summertime. The result is somewhere between crumbly and custardy, with crisp edges thanks to the cheddar, which also helps keep things savory to balance that craveable sweetness.

SERVES 8

For the cornbread

1 stick (½ cup) unsalted butter, melted, plus more for greasing
2 large eggs
1 (15-ounce) can creamed corn
½ cup buttermilk
2 tablespoons date syrup or pure maple syrup
1½ cups all-purpose flour
¾ cup yellow cornmeal
⅓ cup sugar
1½ teaspoons kosher salt
1 tablespoon baking powder
½ cup shredded white cheddar cheese
Kernels from 1 ear corn (optional)

For the date butter

2 sticks (1 cup) salted butter, at room temp
¼ cup date syrup or pure maple syrup

Make the cornbread

Preheat the oven to 375°F. Grease a 10-inch cast-iron skillet or 9-inch square baking dish with a little butter.

In a medium bowl, whisk together the melted butter, eggs, creamed corn, buttermilk, and date syrup. In a separate medium bowl, whisk together the flour, cornmeal, sugar, salt, and baking powder. Add the dry mixture a quarter at a time to the wet mixture and whisk until smooth (no lumps, please!). Fold in the cheddar and corn kernels.

Pour the batter into the greased baking dish and bake, rotating once halfway through, until the cornbread is lightly golden brown on top and a knife inserted into the center comes out clean, 30 to 35 minutes. Let cool slightly while you make the date butter.

Make the date butter and serve

Combine the butter and date syrup in a medium bowl (if using a handheld mixer) or in the bowl of a stand mixer fitted with the whisk attachment. Beat on medium-high speed until smooth and fluffy, a minute or two.

Serve the cornbread hot, with the date butter on the side.

Note: Those molds that make your cornbread look like little half-shucked cobs are very silly—and very cute. If you use them, reduce the baking time to 20 minutes.

Fresh Corn Grits with Truffle Cheese and Romesco

When you heat grated fresh corn, magic happens. All the starch—essentially, naturally occurring cornstarch—thickens the pulp, transforming it into a creamy, textured puree, like intensely corny grits. A little cornmeal, which is optional, adds a bit of welcome heartiness.

Because truffle and corn make the perfect marriage, I fold in sottocenere or another melty, truffle-flecked cheese at the last minute. (If you can't find one, sub Fontina and a teaspoon of trusty Sabatino brand truffle zest.) Romesco, a smoky sauce of peppers and almonds born in Catalonia, sets off the summer sweetness.

SERVES 4

5 ears sweet corn, shucked
1 tablespoon extra-virgin olive oil
1 small shallot, minced
4 garlic cloves, minced
½ cup whole milk
¼ cup heavy cream
2 tablespoons fine grind cornmeal (optional)
1 tablespoon unsalted butter
¾ cup grated sottocenere or another melty, truffle-flecked cheese
1½ teaspoons kosher salt
A few tablespoons Romesco (recipe follows), for garnish (optional)
Thinly sliced fresh chives, for garnish

Cut the kernels off 1 ear of corn and set aside. Grate the other 4 ears of corn on a box grater (use the biggest holes) all the way down to the cob; when you're done, you should have about 2 cups of glorious corn pulp and juice. Set aside.

Heat the olive oil in a medium saucepan over medium-low heat until it shimmers. Add the shallot and garlic and cook, stirring occasionally, until the shallot is soft and translucent but not browned, 3 to 5 minutes.

Add the milk, cream, cornmeal, if desired, and the grated corn pulp and juice. Cook, whisking frequently, until the mixture thickens to the creamy texture of grits or loose polenta, 5 to 8 minutes. Stir in the whole corn kernels and butter, then fold in the cheese, remove the pan from the heat, and let the cheese melt slightly. Season with the salt. Serve garnished with a swirl of romesco, if desired, and a sprinkle of chives.

(continued)

Romesco

MAKES ABOUT 1 CUP

2 guajillo chiles, stemmed, slit open, and seeded
2 garlic cloves, coarsely chopped
1 medium shallot, coarsely chopped
½ cup sliced jarred roasted piquillo peppers
½ cup coarsely chopped unsalted roasted almonds
1 tablespoon sherry vinegar, plus more as needed
2 teaspoons honey
1½ teaspoons smoked paprika
1 teaspoon kosher salt, plus more as needed
Freshly ground black pepper to taste
6 cloves Garlic Confit (page 119) or 2 raw cloves, plus ¼ cup confit oil or olive oil

Heat a small skillet over medium for a minute or so, then add the guajillos and cook, flipping occasionally, until they're fragrant, about 1 minute. Give them a rough chop.

Transfer the guajillos to a food processor along with the remaining ingredients and process, stopping occasionally to scrape down the sides, to a slightly chunky puree. Season to taste with more salt and vinegar.

The romesco will keep in an airtight container in the fridge for up to 5 days.

Corn Pancakes with Bacon, Cotija, and Chile-Scallion Syrup

Pancakes should be sweet, or at least that's how I saw it until I flipped through the *State Bird Provisions* cookbook. There I found a whole chapter devoted to the San Francisco restaurant's obsession with savory pancakes, featuring ingredients like sauerkraut, sablefish, and beef tongue. These aren't *that* savory, but they do blur the line, with the combo of corn, cheddar, and bacon finding a magical middle ground. Even the syrup is brought back from the sugary brink by scallions and chile, making them perfect for brunch (plain or perhaps with a dollop of crème fraîche and fish roe) or dinner (with a simple side of black beans).

MAKES 9

For the syrup

⅔ cup pure maple syrup
1 fairly spicy fresh chile (like a Fresno or serrano), seeded and thinly sliced
Small handful of thinly sliced scallions
½ teaspoon kosher salt
¼ teaspoon freshly ground black pepper

For the pancakes

½ cup all-purpose flour
3 tablespoons fine or medium yellow cornmeal
1½ teaspoons kosher salt
1 teaspoon baking powder
1 teaspoon sugar
½ teaspoon freshly ground black pepper
¼ cup buttermilk
1 tablespoon neutral oil, like canola
2 large eggs
2 cups corn kernels (fresh, thawed frozen, or drained canned)
4 slices cooked bacon, chopped
¼ cup grated cheddar cheese
1 small jalapeño or serrano chile, seeded and diced
3 tablespoons unsalted butter or canola oil
¼ cup or so crumbled Cotija cheese or queso fresco, for serving

(continued)

Make the syrup

Warm the maple syrup in a small saucepan over medium-low heat. Remove from the heat and stir in the chile, scallions, salt, and pepper. Keep warm off the heat.

Make the pancakes

Preheat the oven to 250°F.

In a medium bowl, whisk together the flour, cornmeal, salt, baking powder, sugar, and pepper. In a large bowl, whisk together the buttermilk, oil, and eggs. Add the flour mixture to the egg mixture and whisk until smooth. Stir in the corn, bacon, cheddar, and jalapeño.

Heat the butter or oil in a large skillet over medium-low heat until the butter foams or the oil shimmers. Working in batches, add scoops of the pancake batter (about ¼ cup each). Flatten the scoops a bit and spread out the corn kernels, which tend to clump. Cook, flipping once and giving each a light press, until the pancakes are golden brown on both sides, about 2 minutes per side. Transfer the pancakes to a paper towel–lined baking sheet to drain, then keep warm in the oven. Repeat with the remaining batter.

To serve, top the pancakes with the Cotija and chile-scallion syrup.

Corn Salad with Avocado, Watercress, and Celery Salt Popcorn

Save this recipe for summer corn so good you don't have to cook it. Peppery watercress, juicy cherry tomatoes, and a sharp sherry dressing offset the full-on sweetness of those raw kernels while rich, creamy avocado ties together those contrasting elements. Celery salt–seasoned popcorn for crunch feels much more appropriate than croutons here.

SERVES 4 TO 6

For the dressing

¼ cup sherry vinegar
3 tablespoons extra-virgin olive oil
2 tablespoons honey
2 teaspoons whole-grain mustard
½ teaspoon celery seed
½ teaspoon red chile flakes
1 shallot, minced (about 2 tablespoons)
1 teaspoon kosher salt
Freshly ground black pepper

For the popcorn

2 tablespoons popcorn kernels, freshly popped (about 2 cups)
Extra-virgin olive oil spray or a drizzle of olive oil
¼ teaspoon celery salt, or more to taste

For the salad

¼ red onion, very thinly sliced (a mandoline helps) and soaked in ice water for 20 minutes, then drained
1 ripe but firm Hass avocado, cubed
1 pint mixed cherry tomatoes, halved
Kernels from 2 ears white corn
2 big handfuls of trimmed watercress
Small handful of basil leaves

Make the dressing

Whisk together all the dressing ingredients in a large bowl.

Make the popcorn

Put the popcorn in a medium bowl, spray or drizzle with olive oil, and toss to coat well. Sprinkle on the celery salt and toss to coat well.

Make the salad

Add all the salad ingredients to the bowl with the dressing, gently toss to coat, and transfer to a serving platter. Scatter the popcorn over the salad and serve.

Fresh Baby Corn with Chipotle-Buttermilk Ranch and Tortilla Crumble

For as long as I can remember I've been obsessed with baby corn. As a kid, I adored it, from a can and in plenty of '80s stir-fries, because it's so damn cute. Later I found it fresh at the farmers' market and fell for the flavor—like corn but without the sweetness—and the fact that you can eat the entire thing, cob and all.

I give them just a few minutes on a grill or in a pan to brown, then serve the crunchy, snackable babies with buttermilk ranch, one of the world's perfect condiments, spiked with smoky chipotle. I coat the corn in a simple crumble made from leftover tortillas that reminds me of Corn Nuts. So much so that sometimes I skip the crumble and pulse actual Corn Nuts in the food processor—ranch flavored, if you please.

SERVES 4

For the ranch

½ cup mayonnaise
½ cup sour cream
¼ cup buttermilk
1 teaspoon onion powder
1 teaspoon garlic powder
Large pinch of chopped fresh dill
1 canned chipotle pepper in adobo sauce, finely chopped, plus 1 tablespoon of the adobo
1 teaspoon kosher salt
½ teaspoon freshly ground black pepper

For the tortilla crumble

3 (6-inch) corn tortillas (preferably slightly stale), coarsely chopped
1½ tablespoons neutral oil, like canola
½ teaspoon garlic powder
½ teaspoon smoked paprika
½ teaspoon kosher salt

For the corn

32 ears fresh baby corn, or 4 large ears corn, shucked
2 tablespoons neutral oil, like canola
1½ teaspoons kosher salt
1 teaspoon freshly ground black pepper
1 tablespoon thinly sliced fresh chives, plus more for garnish

Make the ranch

Whisk together all the ranch ingredients in a medium bowl. Cover and refrigerate to let the flavors meld and get it nice and cold, at least 1 hour or, even better, overnight.

Make the tortilla crumble

Preheat the oven to 350°F. Line a baking sheet with parchment paper (or a silicone baking mat, if you have one).

Pulse the tortillas in a food processor until the size of coarse breadcrumbs. Transfer to the prepared baking sheet, then drizzle with the oil, sprinkle with the garlic powder, paprika, and salt, and toss well.

Spread out the crumbs and bake, stirring and rotating the pan halfway through, until the crumbs are golden brown and crisp, 7 to 8 minutes. Set aside.

Make the corn

Put the corn in a large bowl, add the oil, salt, and pepper, and toss to coat. Set a grill pan or large cast-iron pan over medium-high heat. When the pan is hot, add the corn, working in batches if necessary, and cook, rotating the corn occasionally, until browned all over, 3 to 4 minutes. As soon as it's browned, transfer the corn to the pan with the tortilla crumble and roll each piece around to coat in the crumbs as best you can. Sprinkle the chives over the corn.

Stack the corn on a plate, sprinkle with any leftover crumble and some more chives, and serve with the ranch on the side for dipping.

FUN IN THE SUMMERTIME

Peppers, Eggplants, Figs, and More

Black Mission Figs with Pistachio Relish and Warm Chorizo Honey

My parents had a Black Mission fig tree in their yard and now I have one in mine. For most of the year, they're purely ornamental. But for a few weeks in the summer, the branches are heavy with plump, blackish-purple fruit, and neither I nor the squirrels can pick them quickly enough. I walk through a graveyard of fallen figs to bring my haul inside and start the fun project of figuring out how to serve them to anyone and everyone who comes over. I like to take the lusciously sweet fruit in a slightly savory direction, so I drizzle them with honey spiked with porky, spicy chorizo then spoon on a zippy, herby pistachio situation to provide balance and texture.

SERVES 4

½ cup shelled raw unsalted pistachios
¼ cup extra-virgin olive oil, plus more for the chorizo
4 ounces Mexican pork chorizo, casings removed
½ cup honey
1 shallot, minced (about 2 tablespoons)
2 teaspoons sherry vinegar
¼ cup fresh sage leaves, finely chopped
¼ cup fresh flat-leaf parsley (leaves and small stems), finely chopped
1 teaspoon flaky sea salt, like Maldon, or more to taste
Freshly ground black pepper
12 to 15 fresh Black Mission figs, halved or quartered depending on size, at room temp

Preheat the oven to 350°F.

Put the pistachios on a small baking sheet, shake them out into an even layer, and toast in the oven until light golden brown and fragrant, about 5 minutes. Let them cool slightly, then coarsely chop and set aside.

Set a small pan over medium-high heat. Add a splash of olive oil, then the chorizo. Cook, breaking up the sausage into small pieces, until deep golden brown and crispy, about 6 minutes. Turn off the heat, add the honey, and stir to coat the chorizo. Keep warm off the heat.

Stir together the shallot and vinegar in a small bowl and let them sit at room temperature for at least 5 minutes, so the shallot loses some of its sharpness. Stir in the pistachios and olive oil, then fold in the sage and parsley. Season with the flaky salt and pepper to taste.

Arrange the figs cut-side up on a serving platter. Spoon on the chorizo honey, then the pistachio relish, and serve.

Blistered Shishito Peppers with Miso-Tahini Dressing and Garlic Furikake

Once upon a time, these bite-size green peppers were tough to find in the US outside of the occasional farmers' market stall. But as people encountered their pleasures at Japanese restaurants (and Spanish ones, which serve the similar Padrón peppers), they blew up, and nowadays they're all over chef menus and are even sold in bags at the supermarket.

The key, if you ask me, is cooking them hot and quick, so they blister but stay bright green and crisp and retain their nice grassy flavor. (Another fun part is that occasionally, one of the mild peppers turns out to be as hot as a serrano chile.) Here they remain the star of this dish, though the creamy miso-tahini sauce and a garlic-and-sumac-studded sprinkle inspired by the Japanese condiment furikake are so tasty, they threaten to steal the show.

SERVES 4

For the furikake

2 tablespoons neutral oil, like canola
3 garlic cloves, minced
1 sheet nori seaweed (about 8 by 7 inches), finely chopped
¼ cup katsuobushi (bonito flakes), torn, pulsed in a small food processor
¼ cup toasted white sesame seeds, pulsed in a small food processor
1 tablespoon ground sumac
2 teaspoons flaky sea salt, like Maldon

For the dressing

¼ cup well-stirred tahini
1 tablespoon soy sauce
2 teaspoons shiro (white) miso paste
2 teaspoons honey
Finely grated zest and juice of 1 lime
Kosher salt

For the peppers

8 ounces shishito peppers
1 tablespoon neutral oil, like canola

(continued)

Make the furikake

Combine the oil and garlic in a small saucepan, set it over medium heat, and gently fry the garlic, stirring almost constantly, until light golden brown and fragrant, about 2 minutes. Drain the garlic, reserving the tasty oil for the dressing, then spread the garlic on a paper towel to drain and cool. The garlic will continue to brown and crisp as it cools.

Transfer the cooled garlic to a medium bowl and add the nori, katsuobushi, sesame seeds, sumac, and flaky salt. Mix well and set aside. (The furikake will keep in an airtight container in a cool, dry place for up to 2 days.)

Make the dressing

Combine the tahini, soy sauce, miso, honey, lime zest, lime juice, 2 tablespoons water, and the reserved garlic oil in a small bowl and stir until smooth. Season with salt to taste. Set aside.

If the dressing thickens as it sits, stir in 1 teaspoon water at a time until drippy and pourable, then season again with salt.

Make the peppers

Set a large heavy-bottomed pan over high heat. Toss the shishitos with the oil in a medium bowl to evenly coat. When the pan is nice and hot, add the shishitos and shake them out into an even layer. Cook until deeply charred and blistered on the first side, 2 to 3 minutes. Flip the shishitos and cook until crisp-tender and still bright green, 1 to 2 minutes.

Serve the warm shishitos on a plate, topped with the dressing (give it a quick whisk if it has separated) and sprinkled generously with the furikake.

Spaghetti with Zucchini, Prosciutto, and Lemon-Butter Breadcrumbs

My favorite way to eat zucchini goes like this: caramelized on the outside, a slight snap in the center, some garlic, and some lemon. Only problem is, that's not dinner. But *this* is. I toss lots of hard-roasted zucchini (with the seedy core removed to head off any mush) with spaghetti, then add lemony breadcrumbs for texture. A few small touches—ribbons of prosciutto, fresh basil, and fragrant Meyer lemon—level up this perfect weeknight pasta.

SERVES 4

3 medium zucchini, trimmed
4 tablespoons extra-virgin olive oil
Kosher salt
1 pound dried spaghetti
4 medium garlic cloves, thinly sliced
½ teaspoon freshly ground black pepper
½ teaspoon Aleppo pepper or red chile flakes
Finely grated zest and juice of 1 Meyer lemon or regular lemon
2 large handfuls of finely grated Parmesan cheese, plus more for serving
Large handful of basil leaves, sliced or torn at the last minute
6 thin slices of prosciutto, cut into thin strips
Lemon-Butter Breadcrumbs (recipe follows)

Preheat the oven to 400°F.

Quarter the zucchini lengthwise, then slice off and discard the seedy center parts. Cut the zucchini into roughly 3 by ¼-inch batons and transfer to a large bowl. Add 2 tablespoons of the oil and 1½ teaspoons salt and toss to coat. Spread the zucchini in a single layer on a large baking sheet and roast, tossing once, until browned at the edges, 15 to 20 minutes.

Meanwhile, bring a large pot of water to a boil and add a generous handful of salt. Add the pasta and cook, stirring occasionally, until al dente, about 10 minutes. Drain the pasta, reserving about ½ cup of the pasta water.

Combine the remaining 2 tablespoons oil and the garlic in a large skillet or other wide pan and cook over medium-low heat until the garlic gets a little color. Add the pasta, black pepper, and Aleppo pepper, toss well, then add the zucchini and toss gently but well.

Add the lemon zest, lemon juice, Parm, basil, and prosciutto and toss well, gradually adding some of the reserved pasta water to sauce up the noodles. Season with salt to taste and serve topped with the breadcrumbs and more Parmesan.

(continued)

Lemon-Butter Breadcrumbs

MAKES ABOUT ¾ CUP

1 cup torn crustless sourdough bread
3 tablespoons unsalted butter
Finely grated zest of 1 lemon
¼ teaspoon kosher salt
A couple pinches of freshly ground black pepper

Pulse the bread in a food processor into coarse crumbs.

Melt the butter in a medium pan over medium-low heat, then cook until it begins to turn golden brown, 2 to 3 minutes. Add the breadcrumbs and stir to coat in the butter, then stir in the lemon zest, salt, and pepper. Reduce the heat to low and cook, stirring frequently, until the breadcrumbs are golden brown and crispy, 2 to 3 minutes. Transfer the crumbs to a paper towel–lined bowl to drain. Use within 1 hour.

Charred Okra with Sweet and Spicy Harissa Dressing

When it's summertime at Playa, okra is my "send them something" dish. I've found that diners often avoid okra when it's on our menu, but as a big booster of the summertime pods, I'm confident that even skittish eaters will love them if they eat them prepared like this. So when friends come in for dinner or there are VIPs at the bar, I'll send them a plate. And I've yet to see that plate come back anything but clean.

While okra has a reputation for being slimy—which sometimes it is, and wonderfully so—any trace of sliminess is demolished when you halve the pods and give the cut sides a hard sear like I do here. From there, you're a sweet-spicy dressing away from a mind-changing dish.

SERVES 4 TO 6

For the dressing

¼ cup sherry vinegar
2 tablespoons honey
1 tablespoon harissa
1 tablespoon whole-grain mustard
1 Fresno chile or red jalapeño, seeded and minced
1 large garlic clove, grated on a Microplane
1 teaspoon kosher salt
¼ teaspoon freshly ground black pepper
¼ cup extra-virgin olive oil

For the okra

¼ cup neutral oil, like canola
2 pounds small to medium okra pods, stems trimmed, halved lengthwise
Kosher salt

Make the dressing

Whisk together the vinegar, honey, harissa, mustard, chile, garlic, salt, and pepper in a small bowl. While whisking constantly, slowly drizzle in the olive oil. Set aside.

Make the okra

Set a large cast-iron skillet or grill pan over medium-high heat, then add the oil and let it shimmer.

Working in batches to avoid crowding, add the okra to the hot pan, cut-side down, and cook until deeply golden brown on the bottom and crispy at the edges, 4 to 5 minutes. Flip, sprinkle with salt, and cook until the second side gets a little color and the okra is tender but still retains a slight bite, 1 to 2 minutes. (You can also toss the okra with the oil and salt, arrange the okra cut-side down in a single layer on a large baking sheet, and roast at 400°F on the center rack, rotating the baking sheet once halfway through, for about 15 minutes.)

Transfer the okra to a serving plate. Season to taste with salt, spoon on about ½ cup of the dressing (give it a quick whisk if it has separated) or more to taste, and serve immediately.

Fairy Tale Eggplant with Pink Peppercorn Chimichurri

This is for anyone who has ever ogled a pile of tiny eggplant at the farmers' market then kept walking, wondering what to do with these miniature glossy black or striped purple beauties. My strategy is: not much. I cook them hot—they contain less water than their larger counterparts, so they caramelize especially well—then finish them in the oven so the flesh is creamy. Chimichurri, a zippy, herby sauce from Argentina, is the perfect accompaniment, and I spike mine with the unexpected floral bite of pink peppercorns.

If you can't find Fairy Tale eggplants, then use Japanese or Italian eggplants, halved lengthwise then cut crosswise into roughly 2-inch pieces.

SERVES 4

For the chimichurri

2 tablespoons whole pink peppercorns
1 small shallot, minced
¼ cup red wine vinegar
½ cup extra-virgin olive oil
¼ teaspoon sugar
3 garlic cloves, grated on a Microplane
2 teaspoons kosher salt
2 big handfuls of mixed cilantro, parsley, and mint, finely chopped
Small handful of oregano leaves, finely chopped

For the eggplant

3 pounds Fairy Tale eggplants, stemmed and halved lengthwise
1½ tablespoons kosher salt
2 tablespoons neutral oil, like canola, plus more as needed
Flaky sea salt, like Maldon
Store-bought fried garlic, for garnish (optional)

Make the chimichurri

Preheat the oven to 350°F.

Spread the peppercorns on a small baking sheet and pop it in the oven to toast until warm and fragrant, 2 to 3 minutes. Remove from the oven and let cool (keep the oven on), then coarsely grind them in a blender or spice grinder or with a mortar and pestle.

Combine the shallot and vinegar in a medium bowl and let stand for 5 minutes to tame the shallot's raw bite. Add the olive oil, sugar, garlic, and salt, stir well, then add the mixed herbs, oregano, and pink peppercorns and stir once more. Set aside.

Cook the eggplant

Season the eggplants with the salt and let sit at room temperature until they release some moisture, 15 to 20 minutes. Blot dry with paper towels.

Heat 2 tablespoons of the oil in a large cast-iron pan over medium heat until it shimmers. Working in batches to avoid crowding, add the eggplant halves, cut-side down, and cook until golden brown on the bottom, 2 to 3 minutes. Transfer to a large baking sheet, cut-side up and in a single layer. Repeat with the remaining eggplant, adding more oil to the pan as needed.

Transfer the baking sheet to the oven and roast the eggplant until the flesh is fully tender, 25 to 35 minutes.

Transfer to a serving platter and add a nice sprinkle of flaky salt. Spoon the chimichurri over the eggplants, sprinkle on the fried garlic, and serve. They're great warm or at room temp.

Summer Veggie Fideuà

I can't get enough of the variation on paella for which Spanish cooks swap out rice for fideos—short thin noodles that soak up the briny stock and develop a crisp crust on the bottom. I order fideuà (I looked it up: it's *fee-DEY-wah*) whenever I see it and make it often at home. It's perfect for entertaining—you can cook it before friends arrive then pop it in the oven to crisp up just before serving. And it's a fantastic way to use up whatever summer vegetables are in your fridge or garden and take them from side dish to centerpiece.

SERVES 4 TO 6

- 1 orange bell pepper, cut into ¼-inch-thick strips
- 2 medium zucchini, cut to match the pepper strips
- 2 medium summer squash, cut to match the pepper strips
- 2 medium Japanese eggplants, cut into ¼- to ½-inch-thick rounds
- Extra-virgin olive oil
- Kosher salt and freshly ground black pepper
- 1 pound dried fideos or dried angel hair pasta, broken into 2-inch-ish pieces
- 3 garlic cloves, thinly sliced
- 1 large shallot, thinly sliced
- 2 tablespoons tomato paste
- 2 teaspoons crushed Calabrian chile or red chile flakes
- ¼ cup dry white wine
- 3½ to 4 cups shellfish stock (e.g., lobster or shrimp stock) or clam juice
- Kernels from 2 ears white corn
- ¼ cup sliced jarred roasted piquillo peppers
- 2 tablespoons unsalted butter
- Finely grated zest and juice of 1 lemon
- Aioli (recipe follows), for serving
- Sliced basil leaves, for garnish

Preheat the oven to 375°F.

Put the bell pepper, zucchini, summer squash, and eggplants on a large baking sheet, drizzle with 2 tablespoons olive oil, and season lightly with salt and black pepper. Toss to coat the vegetables in the oil, then spread them out into an even layer. Roast, stirring the vegetables halfway through, until they're golden brown and tender, 25 to 35 minutes. Remove from the oven but leave the oven on.

Set a 14- to 16-inch paella pan or cast-iron skillet over medium-high heat. Add 1 tablespoon olive oil and swirl the pan to coat. Add the fideos, stir to coat them with oil, and cook, stirring almost constantly, until light golden brown and fragrant, 1 to 2 minutes. Add the garlic, shallot, and a pinch of salt and cook, stirring frequently, until fragrant, 30 seconds to 1 minute more.

Add the tomato paste and cook, stirring constantly, until it darkens a bit and begins to dry out, 1 to 2 minutes. Stir in the Calabrian chile. Add the wine and stir, scraping up all the tasty browned bits from the bottom of the pan with a wooden spoon. Add half the stock, stir, and let it come to a simmer. Cover and cook, stirring occasionally, until the fideos are very al dente, about 5 minutes.

Remove the lid and mix in the roasted veggies, corn kernels, piquillo peppers, butter, lemon zest, lemon juice, and remaining stock and let the mixture return to a simmer. Taste and add more salt if needed—it should taste like a broth you'd be happy to eat.

Transfer the pan to the oven and bake, uncovered, until the liquid has been fully absorbed, about 15 minutes. Then keep baking until the bottom is crusty and golden (dip a spoon in and take a peek to check), 25 to 30 minutes more.

Serve straight out of the pan, dolloped with aioli and sprinkled with basil.

(continued)

Aioli

¼ cup cloves Garlic Confit (page 119) or 2 raw cloves, plus ½ cup confit oil or olive oil
1 large egg yolk
2 tablespoons Meyer lemon juice or regular lemon juice
1 teaspoon Dijon mustard
Dash of Tabasco
1 teaspoon kosher salt, plus more as needed
¼ cup neutral oil, like canola

Combine the garlic confit (but not the oil just yet), egg yolk, lemon juice, mustard, Tabasco, and salt in a small food processor and buzz until smooth. With the processor running, drizzle in the neutral oil and confit oil. Add 1 teaspoon water and process until smooth, then season to taste with more salt. The aioli will keep in an airtight container in the fridge for up to 5 days.

Sweet and Sour Eggplant with Peanuts, Coriander, and Sichuan Peppercorns

For my second job as an executive chef, I inherited a staff but scrapped the entire menu. Well, everything except for this one Italian-inspired eggplant dish prepared agrodolce, bracingly sweet and sour from a soak in a mixture of vinegar and sugar. It was that good. Twenty-five years later, I still riff on the dish all the time, and this might be my favorite rendition. Vinegar and honey team up with the lip-buzzing delight of Sichuan peppercorns. Peanuts and whole coriander seeds provide texture and pops of flavor, while lime juice and cilantro freshen it all up.

SERVES 4

For the sweet and sour

2 teaspoons coriander seeds
2 teaspoons Sichuan peppercorns
3 tablespoons apple cider vinegar
3 tablespoons honey
1 teaspoon gochugaru (Korean chile flakes) or crushed Calabrian chile

For the eggplants

2 tablespoons coconut oil or neutral oil, like canola
2 pounds Japanese eggplants, halved lengthwise and cut crosswise on an angle into ½-inch-thick pieces
½ cup thinly sliced red onion
2 garlic cloves, thinly sliced
Kosher salt and freshly ground black pepper
1 teaspoon toasted sesame oil
1 tablespoon thinly sliced cilantro stems, plus a big pinch of leaves for garnish
Finely grated zest and juice of 1 lime
Coarsely chopped roasted unsalted peanuts (I love skin-on Spanish peanuts), for serving

Make the sweet and sour

Set a small pan over medium-high heat, add the coriander seeds, and toast, shaking the pan occasionally, until fragrant, about 2 minutes. Transfer to a small bowl and set aside.

In the same pan, toast the Sichuan peppercorns, shaking the pan occasionally, until fragrant, about 2 minutes. Coarsely grind the peppercorns in a spice grinder and transfer to a separate small bowl. Add the vinegar, honey, and chile flakes to the bowl with the peppercorns, stir well, and set aside.

(continued)

Make the eggplants

Heat half of the coconut oil in a heavy-bottomed 14-inch skillet (or work in two batches with a smaller skillet) over medium-high heat until it shimmers. Add half of the eggplant and cook, turning occasionally, until golden brown and nearly tender, 5 to 7 minutes. Transfer to a plate and repeat with the remaining coconut oil and eggplant.

Return the eggplant to the skillet, then stir in the toasted coriander seeds, onion, and garlic and season with 2 teaspoons salt and pepper to taste. Cook until the onion begins to soften and the eggplant is tender, 3 to 5 minutes.

Add the sweet and sour mixture, stir gently but well, and cook for 20 seconds or so, so the syrupy sauce coats the eggplant. Drizzle in the sesame oil and remove the pan from the heat. Add the cilantro stems, lime zest, and lime juice and mix gently but well. Season to taste with more salt.

Transfer to a plate, garnish with the cilantro leaves and peanuts, and serve right away.

Watermelon "Greek Salad" with Creamy Feta and Olive Brine Dressing

Super-sweet watermelon begs for balance. A little heat from fresh chiles, some salty olives, and tangy feta do the trick. And while cubes of the cheese are lovely, I take a tip from my dear friend Casey Thompson, a fellow contestant on *Top Chef*, the actual top chef at the awesome Folktable Restaurant in Sonoma, California, and a consistent source of inspiration for me: I buzz it with yogurt to make a luxe bed (with 300-thread-count sheets) for juicy cubes of summer fruit.

SERVES 4

For the creamy feta

¾ cup plain full-fat Greek yogurt or labneh
8 ounces feta cheese, coarsely crumbled
1 garlic clove, coarsely chopped
2 tablespoons extra-virgin olive oil
1 teaspoon kosher salt

For the dressing

1 small shallot, minced
2 tablespoons Kalamata olive brine
2 teaspoons Dijon mustard
2 teaspoons whole-grain mustard
1 tablespoon honey
2 tablespoons red wine vinegar
1 tablespoon finely chopped fresh oregano leaves, or 1 teaspoon dried
1 teaspoon kosher salt
Freshly ground black pepper
⅓ cup extra-virgin olive oil

For the salad

1 small ripe seedless red watermelon, rind removed, cut into ½-inch cubes (about 3 cups)
½ English cucumber, seeded and julienned
½ cup pitted Kalamata olives, halved or quartered
½ cup thinly sliced red onion, soaked in ice water for 5 minutes, then drained
1 or 2 Fresno chiles, seeded and julienned
1 tablespoon fresh oregano leaves
Salted toasted sunflower seeds, for sprinkling
Flaky sea salt, like Maldon
Freshly ground black pepper
Extra-virgin olive oil

Make the creamy feta

Put the yogurt, feta, garlic, olive oil, and salt in a mini food processor and process, stopping to occasionally scrape down the sides, until completely smooth.

Make the dressing

Whisk together the shallot, olive brine, mustards, honey, vinegar, oregano, salt, and pepper to taste in a small bowl. While whisking constantly, slowly drizzle in the olive oil.

Make the salad

Spoon the cheese mixture into a large, wide serving bowl or platter, then scatter on the watermelon. Toss the cucumbers, olives, onion, chiles, and oregano with about half the dressing and scatter the vegetables on top of the watermelon. Spoon on more dressing to taste, then sprinkle with the sunflower seeds, flaky salt, and pepper to taste. Drizzle with olive oil and serve.

BONUS COCKTAIL:
Watermelon-Hibiscus Rum Punch

MAKES 8 TO 10 DRINKS

For the hibiscus syrup

½ cup sugar

¼ cup dried hibiscus flowers or loose hibiscus tea

For the punch

32 ounces (4 cups) chilled watermelon juice, store-bought or homemade (see Note)

16 ounces (2 cups) light rum

2 ounces (¼ cup) Meyer lemon juice or regular lemon juice

2 ounces (¼ cup) fresh lime juice

1 lime, very thinly sliced

1 Meyer lemon or regular lemon, very thinly sliced

Handful of mint leaves

Ice cubes

Make the syrup

Combine the sugar, hibiscus, and ½ cup water in a small saucepan, stir, and bring to a boil over medium-high heat. Turn off the heat and set aside to steep for 15 minutes or so, stirring to make sure the sugar has fully dissolved. Strain into a container, cover, and refrigerate until chilled before using, about 1 hour. (The syrup will keep in the fridge for up to 1 week.)

Make the punch

Combine the watermelon juice, rum, lemon juice, lime juice, and ¾ cup of the hibiscus syrup in a punch bowl or large pitcher and stir well to combine. Add 2 cups of ice cubes and stir well to chill the punch. Add the lime and lemon slices and mint and serve.

Note: Look for fresh bottled watermelon juice at markets like Whole Foods, or whip some up yourself: Blend 6 cups cubed or coarsely chopped seeded watermelon, then pour through a fine-mesh strainer into a container. You should have about 4 cups juice.

Muhammara with Pomegranate-Walnut Relish

Summer is pepper-roasting season, when the hot-weather vegetable is at its best. And while I rarely tire of peppers simply charred and marinated with vinegar and oil, I frequently look to the Middle Eastern dip called muhammara as a way to celebrate a glorious glut. Born in Syria, the showstopping puree features sweet, smoky roasted peppers and the texture and flavor-carrying fat of walnuts along with spices like cumin and coriander and dark, tangy pomegranate molasses. It's traditional as part of a spread. At my house, it's often the main event, so I top it with a relish made from pomegranate seeds, crunchy chopped walnuts, and herbs to add texture and brightness. Warm pita or charred crusty bread makes it a meal.

SERVES 4

For the muhammara

2 medium red bell peppers
1¾ cups walnuts
1 cup packed jarred roasted piquillo peppers
½ cup cloves Garlic Confit (recipe follows) or 4 raw peeled cloves
¼ cup lemon juice
¼ cup pomegranate molasses
2 tablespoons apple cider vinegar
2 tablespoons sweet paprika
1 tablespoon honey
2 teaspoons kosher salt, plus more as needed
1 teaspoon ground coriander
1 teaspoon ground cumin
½ teaspoon Aleppo pepper
3 garlic cloves, coarsely chopped
¼ cup panko breadcrumbs (or sub in stale, crustless country or white bread)
½ cup extra-virgin olive oil
½ cup well-stirred tahini

For the relish

½ cup pomegranate seeds
2 tablespoons extra-virgin olive oil, plus more for serving
1 tablespoon pomegranate molasses
1 teaspoon toasted sesame seeds, plus more for serving
1 teaspoon kosher salt, plus more as needed
½ teaspoon ground coriander
½ teaspoon Aleppo pepper, plus more for serving
Big pinch of chopped fresh parsley
Big pinch of thinly sliced fresh chives

Make the muhammara

Roast the bell peppers under the broiler or directly over the flame of a gas stovetop, turning occasionally, until blistered and charred all over, 8 to 10 minutes. Transfer to a medium bowl, cover tightly, and let them cool. Pull off the stems and quarter the peppers. Wipe off the skins and discard the seeds and veins.

(continued)

Preheat the oven to 350°F.

Spread the walnuts on a small baking sheet and toast in the oven, shaking the pan once or twice, until light golden brown and crisp, 5 to 8 minutes. Remove from the oven and set aside.

Put the roasted bell peppers in a food processor along with the piquillo peppers, garlic confit, lemon juice, pomegranate molasses, vinegar, paprika, honey, salt, coriander, cumin, Aleppo pepper, and chopped garlic. Process until smooth. Scoop about half the mixture into a bowl and set aside. Add ¾ cup of the walnuts (reserve the rest for the relish) and the breadcrumbs to the food processor and process to a coarse puree. Return the reserved pepper mixture to the processor and pulse to combine.

Scrape down the sides of the processor, then add the olive oil and tahini and process until smooth. Season to taste with salt. Scrape the muhammara into a serving dish and set aside while you make the relish so the flavors have a chance to meld.

Make the relish

Coarsely chop the remaining 1 cup toasted walnuts and put them in a medium bowl. Add the pomegranate seeds, olive oil, molasses, sesame seeds, salt, coriander, Aleppo pepper, parsley, and chives and toss well. Season to taste with salt.

Spoon the relish over the muhammara. Drizzle with more olive oil and sprinkle with more Aleppo pepper and sesame seeds. Serve right away.

Garlic Confit (and Garlic Oil!)

MAKES 1 CUP GARLIC CLOVES AND 1½ CUPS CONFIT OIL

2 cups garlic cloves (from about 6 heads)
½ teaspoon kosher salt
3 thyme sprigs
1 rosemary sprig
1½ cups olive oil (you're not necessary here, extra-virgin), plus more if necessary

Preheat the oven to 325°F.

Combine the garlic, salt, thyme, and rosemary in a small, narrow ovenproof pot (a small loaf pan works nicely) and add the olive oil, using more, if necessary, to just submerge the cloves. Cover the pot with a lid or aluminum foil, place it in the oven, and cook, without stirring, until the cloves are smoosh-ably soft (you're not looking for much, if any, color), 45 minutes to 1 hour. Let cool completely. Transfer the garlic cloves and confit oil to an airtight container and store in the fridge for up to 3 weeks.

GREENS

Crisp, Creamy, Steamy

Green Curry Greens with Mung Beans

By the look of these creamed greens, you'd expect them to taste cozy and mild. Then you take a bite. Instead of cream and a touch of garlic, you get a punch of green curry, the rich sweetness of coconut milk, and the brightness of lime, with mung beans providing little pops of texture. It's a fantastic, and unexpected, way to exalt gorgeous greens from the market or to revive whatever's wilting in your fridge.

SERVES 4

2 tablespoons coconut oil
2 large shallots, thinly sliced
4 garlic cloves, grated on a Microplane
2 teaspoons grated fresh ginger
3 tablespoons Thai green curry paste (the Maesri brand is solid)
2 tablespoons light brown sugar
2 teaspoons fish sauce
1 tablespoon kosher salt
2 (13.5-ounce) cans full-fat coconut milk
2 pounds mixed hearty greens (like kale, mustard, and collard greens), thick stems and ribs discarded, and coarsely chopped
1½ cups cooked mung beans
1 big handful of basil leaves, coarsely chopped at the last minute
Juice of 1 lime, plus more to taste

Heat the coconut oil in a large Dutch oven over medium until it shimmers. Add the shallots and cook, stirring occasionally, until they begin to brown, 3 to 5 minutes. Add the garlic and ginger and cook, stirring frequently, just until they're fragrant and pick up a little color, a minute or two.

Add the curry paste, brown sugar, fish sauce, and salt and stir well, then stir in the coconut milk. Bring the mixture to a simmer. Add the greens, toss well with tongs, then cover and cook, tossing occasionally, until they fully wilt, 3 to 4 minutes.

Transfer about a third of the greens to a blender, leaving the rest of them covered and simmering in the pot. Add ¼ cup water to the blender, puree the greens until they're completely smooth, and pour back into the pot.

Stir in the mung beans and basil, increase the heat slightly, and simmer, uncovered, until the liquid thickens to a sauce, 8 to 10 minutes. Stir in the lime juice, season to taste with more salt and lime juice, and serve.

Kale Gnudi with Brown Butter, Green Apple, and Preserved Lemon

Gnudi are one of my go-tos in competition, just the thing when I need to cook a quick and easy dish that also feels grand and impressive. Named for the Italian word for "naked," they're essentially the ricotta filling for ravioli stripped of their pasta covering and bound by a little flour. I pack in loads of kale to make these fluffy pillows green and flavorful. And while you can sauce them however you'd like—pesto, marinara, bacon broth (page 47)—this combination of brown butter and apple, preserved lemon and rosemary hits all of your palate's pleasure points.

SERVES 4

For the gnudi

Kosher salt

1 large bunch curly kale (about ½ pound), stemmed and coarsely chopped

2 cups whole-milk ricotta cheese

2 large egg yolks

½ cup finely grated Parmesan cheese

1½ teaspoons kosher salt, plus more for the pasta water

¼ teaspoon freshly grated nutmeg

1½ cups all-purpose flour, plus more for dusting

For the dish

½ stick (4 tablespoons) unsalted butter

1 green apple, peeled, cored, and diced into ¼ inch pieces right before cooking

1 medium shallot, minced

1 teaspoon kosher salt

1 cup unsalted chicken stock

Thinly sliced peel from ½ preserved lemon

2 teaspoons whole-grain mustard

1 teaspoon lemon juice

¼ teaspoon finely chopped fresh rosemary

½ teaspoon freshly ground black pepper

¼ cup pine nuts, toasted

Freshly grated Parmesan cheese, for serving

Make the gnudi

Bring a large pot of water to a boil and salt it heavily so it tastes like the sea. Fill a large bowl with ice and water. Add the kale to the boiling water and cook until tender (a leaf should tear easily), 2 to 3 minutes. Transfer to the ice water to cool completely, then drain and squeeze to remove excess water. Reserve the pot of cooking water, scooping out any lingering bits of kale.

Transfer the kale to a food processor and pulse until it's finely chopped. Add the ricotta, egg yolks, Parmesan, salt, and nutmeg and pulse until everything is combined. Transfer the mixture to a large bowl and add the flour. Gently mix with your hands until the mixture comes together into a uniform dough, gradually adding additional flour if the dough sticks to your fingers.

(continued)

Lightly dust a large baking sheet with some flour. Dump the dough out onto a floured work surface and cut it into 4 roughly equal pieces. Roll each piece of dough into a 1-inch-wide log and cut the log crosswise into rectangular pieces (gnudi!) that are slightly longer than they are wide. Put the gnudi on the floured baking sheet. They can hang out there for up to an hour before you cook them.

Cook the gnudi

Bring the pot of water back to a boil. Lightly grease a separate baking sheet with some olive oil (that's where the cooked gnudi will go).

Working in two batches, dust off any excess flour from the gnudi, gently drop a few at a time into the boiling water, and give them a stir so they don't stick to the bottom. Cook just until they float to the surface, 90 seconds to 2 minutes. Use a slotted spoon to transfer the gnudi to the oiled baking sheet in a single layer. Repeat with the second batch.

Finish the dish

Set the largest skillet you have over medium-high heat. Add the butter and cook until it turns a nutty brown color, 1 to 2 minutes. Add the gnudi to the pan and cook, flipping once, until they're golden brown on both sides, 2 to 3 minutes. Use a slotted spoon to transfer them back to the baking sheet.

Add the apples and shallot to the skillet and cook, stirring occasionally, until the shallot begins to brown, 2 to 3 minutes. Sprinkle on the salt, then add the stock, preserved lemon peel, mustard, lemon juice, and rosemary and let it bubble away, stirring occasionally, until it thickens slightly and looks saucy, not brothy, 2 to 4 minutes.

Turn off the heat. Stir in the pepper, then return the gnudi to the skillet, add the pine nuts, and toss gently but well. Transfer to a big, shallow serving bowl, grate some Parmesan over the top, and serve.

Note: I love to garnish the dish with a little fried rosemary. Get a few glugs of olive oil hot over medium-high heat in a skillet, tip the pan so it pools, and add a few pinches of rosemary leaves. Fry for a few seconds until crispy, then transfer to paper towels to drain and sprinkle with salt.

Braised Greens with Tomato, Mortadella, and Olives

This bowl of saucy braised greens is extra special. Kale and escarole cook down until they're tender but not melty, and their dueling textures and flavors, one a little sweet and the other a little bitter, keep things interesting. The fireworks come from briny green olives, caramelized onions, and crisp-edged mortadella. The sophisticated Italian forefather of American bologna, mortadella is rarely cooked. Yet it's almost always in my fridge (my son, Hudson, can't get enough), and its texture here is just awesome.

With some grilled crusty bread on the side or garlicky breadcrumbs on top, these greens are a one-dish dinner.

SERVES 4

- 2 tablespoons unsalted butter
- 2 tablespoons extra-virgin olive oil
- 4 ounces sliced mortadella, cut into ½-inch-wide strips
- 2 yellow onions, sliced into thin half-moons
- 2 teaspoons light brown sugar
- 1½ teaspoons kosher salt, plus more as needed
- 3 tablespoons tomato paste
- 1 teaspoon crushed Calabrian chile, or ½ teaspoon red chile flakes
- 2 cups unsalted chicken stock
- 2 teaspoons colatura (Italian anchovy sauce) or fish sauce
- 1 pound Tuscan kale or other kale (about 2 bunches), stemmed and very coarsely chopped
- 1 pound escarole (1 large head), trimmed and coarsely chopped
- 8 ounces watercress or other peppery greens, woody stems removed
- ½ cup coarsely chopped pitted green olives (I like Castelvetrano here)

Heat the butter and olive oil in a large Dutch oven over medium-low heat until the butter melts. Add the mortadella and cook, stirring frequently, until the edges are golden and slightly crisp, 2 to 3 minutes. Remove the mortadella with a slotted spoon and set aside.

Add the onions, brown sugar, and 1 teaspoon of the salt to the pot and increase the heat to medium. Cook, stirring frequently and adding a splash of water if the onions threaten to burn, until the onions turn caramel brown and fully soft but not jammy, 15 to 20 minutes.

Stir in the tomato paste and Calabrian chile and cook, stirring constantly, until they darken a bit and begin to dry out, 1 to 2 minutes. Add the stock, colatura, and remaining ½ teaspoon salt and stir, scraping up any browned bits from the bottom of the pot.

Add the kale, escarole, and watercress. Raise the heat to medium-high, cover, and bring to a boil. Reduce the heat to maintain a gentle simmer and cook, stirring occasionally, until the greens are wilted and just tender, 8 to 10 minutes. Uncover and simmer vigorously until the liquid goes from brothy to saucy, 10 to 15 minutes. Stir in the olives and mortadella and cook for a minute more. Season with salt to taste and serve.

Grilled Treviso with Citrus, Smoked Almonds, and Ricotta Salata

People say opposites attract. I say opposites make for a great salad. This one, for instance, is all about contrasts. Treviso that's deeply charred at the edges but fresh and crunchy throughout. Its aggressively bitter flavor juxtaposed with sweet, spicy honey and sharp, salty cheese. Bright, juicy citrus alongside crunchy smoked almonds. (I don't typically buy prepared nuts for anything other than snacking, but they conjure a cooked-over-live-fire feel that's magic here.) Each bite is different. Each bite is perfect.

SERVES 4

For the dressing

2 to 4 mixed sweet citrus fruits (depending on the size), like oranges, tangerines, or red grapefruits
2 tablespoons extra-virgin olive oil
1 tablespoon sherry vinegar
½ teaspoon kosher salt, plus more for seasoning
⅛ teaspoon freshly ground black pepper
1 medium shallot, minced
Handful of parsley, chopped

For the salad

2 tablespoons honey
¼ teaspoon Kashmiri chili powder or cayenne pepper
4 heads Treviso (about 1 pound)
3 tablespoons extra-virgin olive oil
1½ teaspoons kosher salt
½ teaspoon freshly ground black pepper, plus more as needed
¼ cup chopped roasted salted smoked almonds
2 ounces ricotta salata cheese, shaved with a vegetable peeler
Flaky sea salt, like Maldon

Make the dressing

Cut the ends off each citrus fruit to reveal the flesh, then carve off the peel and pith. Holding one fruit over a medium bowl, cut the segments from the membranes, letting them fall into the bowl. When you're done, squeeze in the juice from the membranes. Repeat with the remaining fruit.

Add the olive oil to the bowl, along with the vinegar, salt, pepper, shallot, and parsley. Toss gently but well and set aside in the fridge.

Make the salad

Prepare a grill to cook with high heat. Alternatively, set a grill pan over high heat. Stir together the honey and chili powder in a small microwave-safe bowl and microwave just until the honey is warm.

Trim the root ends of the Treviso, but leave them intact so the heads stay together. Cut each head in half lengthwise and remove any wilted outer leaves. Brush the cut sides of the Treviso with the olive oil and season with the salt and pepper.

Grill, cut-side down, until charred, 3 to 4 minutes. Flip and cook just until the other side is nicely brown and very slightly softened, 3 to 4 minutes more. Transfer the Treviso, cut-side up, to a serving platter.

Give the dressing another toss or two, then spoon it on. Sprinkle on the almonds and ricotta salata, and drizzle on the hot honey. Add flaky salt and some more pepper to taste.

Mom's Endive and Apple Salad with Pine Nuts and Gorgonzola

This is Mom's salad, her secret weapon. Not only was it très chic back in the days when *Heathers* was in theaters, but it was also sturdy enough to sit around for hours, fully dressed, on the holiday table and so good it earned raves from the whole family.

It always had toasted pine nuts and julienned apple. It always had a dressing with lots of shallots and whole-grain mustard but not a lot of oil (at the time, all fats, including olive oil, were considered *baaad*), so it was especially pungent. And it almost always had Gorgonzola—except early on when I begged her to leave it off because, ew blue cheese. And she did until she finally told me to suck it up. She was right. The creamy cheese with its sharp tang ties it all together.

SERVES 4 TO 6

For the dressing

¼ cup sherry vinegar
2 tablespoons honey
1½ tablespoons lemon juice
1½ tablespoons whole-grain mustard
1 medium shallot, minced
1 teaspoon kosher salt, plus more as needed
½ teaspoon freshly ground black pepper, plus more as needed
⅓ cup extra-virgin olive oil

For the salad

2 heads red endive, sliced crosswise about 1 inch thick
2 heads Belgian endive, sliced crosswise about 1 inch thick
1 green apple, cored and cut into thin matchsticks
Small handful of parsley leaves
Small handful of tender celery leaves (or more parsley)
½ cup crumbled Gorgonzola or any aged blue cheese
¼ cup pine nuts, toasted

Make the dressing

Combine the vinegar, honey, lemon juice, mustard, shallot, salt, and pepper in a medium bowl. While whisking constantly, slowly drizzle in the olive oil. Season with more salt and pepper to taste.

Make the salad

Combine the endives, apple, parsley, and celery leaves in a large serving bowl. Drizzle on half the dressing and toss to coat. Taste and add more dressing if you want. Sprinkle the Gorgonzola and pine nuts over the top and serve.

Collard Slaw with Asian Pear and Kohlrabi

Cabbage is usually the hero of slaw, but here that title goes to collard greens. Thinly sliced and uncooked, they absorb the sweet spicy dressing supercharged with fish sauce and miso in a way that cabbage just can't. Collards lack crunch, though, and that's where the sidekicks pick up the slack: kohlrabi with its peppery snap, and Asian pear with its floral sweetness and juicy crispness.

SERVES 4 TO 6

For the dressing

2 tablespoons fish sauce
2 tablespoons unseasoned rice vinegar
2 tablespoons toasted sesame oil
1 tablespoon plus 1 teaspoon honey
1 tablespoon shiro (white) miso paste
1 tablespoon Tabasco or Crystal hot sauce
1 tablespoon toasted sesame seeds
Zest and juice of 1 lime
2 garlic cloves, grated on a Microplane

For the salad

1½ pounds collard greens, center ribs removed, leaves thinly sliced (about 4 quarts)
1 large kohlrabi (about 12 ounces), peeled and cut into thin matchsticks (about 3 cups)
1 large Asian pear, peeled, cored, and cut into thin matchsticks
4 scallions, thinly sliced on an angle
2 Fresno or other moderately hot chiles, seeded and julienned
Flaky sea salt, like Maldon

Make the dressing

Whisk together all the dressing ingredients in a large bowl until well combined.

Make the salad

Add the collards to the bowl with the dressing, toss to coat, and let them marinate in the fridge for at least 15 minutes or up to an hour.

Add the kohlrabi, pear, scallions, and chiles, season with flaky salt (1 to 2 teaspoons), and toss to combine. Serve on a platter.

Little Gems with Persimmon, Sesame Cashews, and Tahini Green Goddess

When my friend, fellow *Top Chef* contestant, and current *Top Chef* host Kristen Kish had this salad at Playa Provisions, she told me it should never leave the menu. You got it, chef! We'll keep tossing Little Gem lettuces (the perfect balance of leafy and crunchy) and slices of Fuyu persimmon (like the love child of cantaloupe and kabocha) in vibrant green goddess dressing enhanced with nutty tahini and sprinkling on these seriously snackable candied cashews.

SERVES 4

For the cashews

3 tablespoons honey
2 tablespoons sugar
1 tablespoon raw sesame seeds
1 teaspoon flaky sea salt, like Maldon
¼ teaspoon cayenne pepper
1 cup unsalted roasted cashews

For the dressing

¼ cup well-stirred tahini
¼ cup lemon juice
3 tablespoons red wine vinegar
1 tablespoon honey
1 tablespoon drained capers
1½ teaspoons kosher salt, plus more as needed
⅛ teaspoon freshly ground black pepper
3 scallions, coarsely chopped
2 garlic cloves, coarsely chopped
½ ripe medium Hass avocado
2 big handfuls of coarsely chopped mixed herbs (parsley, cilantro, mint, a little tarragon)

For the salad

4 small heads Little Gem lettuce, bottoms trimmed and leaves separated
1 large ripe Fuyu persimmon, peeled and thinly sliced into half-moons

Make the cashews

Preheat the oven to 325°F. Line a small baking sheet with parchment paper (or a silicone baking mat, if you have one).

Put the honey in a microwave-safe medium bowl and microwave just until the honey starts to bubble. Stir in 1 tablespoon of the sugar, the sesame seeds, flaky salt, and cayenne. Add the cashews and stir to coat.

Spread the cashews in a single layer on the prepared baking sheet and bake, stirring occasionally, until they're dark golden brown, 10 to 12 minutes. Remove the pan from the oven, sprinkle the cashews with the remaining 1 tablespoon sugar, and toss to coat. Let the cashews cool completely, then give them a rough chop.

Make the dressing

Combine all the dressing ingredients in a blender with ¼ cup water and blend until smooth, gradually adding up to 3 tablespoons of additional water if needed to get the machine going. Season with more salt to taste. The dressing keeps its bright color for up to 1 hour.

Make the salad

Put the lettuce and persimmon in a large salad bowl. Add most of the dressing (give it a quick whisk if it has separated) and toss to coat, then add the rest of the dressing if you'd like. Toss in most of the cashews, sprinkle the rest over the top, and serve.

Black Garlic Caesar with Poached Egg and Crispy Parmesan

As a restless chef, sometimes you want to break things, then piece them back together to create a dish that feels new but builds on the fundamentals that made the original so good in the first place. For example, this fun riff on Caesar. I stick with the punchy dressing of the classic, and rev up the funk and umami with fermented black garlic. I keep the crisp lettuce, but use bold, hearty chicories, like radicchio and escarole. Crisp shards of Parmesan echo the crunch of traditional croutons, and I steal the egg from the dressing, poach it, and perch it on top, letting the runny yolk coat the leafy greens.

SERVES 4

For the dressing

3 tablespoons red wine vinegar
2 tablespoons grated Parmesan cheese
1 tablespoon drained capers
2 teaspoons Dijon mustard
Juice of 1 lemon
5 oil-packed anchovy fillets, drained
5 black garlic cloves, peeled
2 garlic cloves, coarsely chopped
Lots of freshly ground black pepper
½ teaspoon kosher salt
¼ cup extra-virgin olive oil

For the Parmesan crumbs

Nonstick cooking spray
¾ cup finely grated Parmesan cheese
Freshly ground black pepper

For the salad

1 tablespoon distilled white vinegar
4 large eggs
A few pinches of kosher salt
8 cups torn trimmed hardy greens (like chicories, stemmed kale leaves, and romaine)
Extra-virgin olive oil
A few pinches of flaky sea salt, like Maldon

Make the dressing

Combine the vinegar, Parmesan, capers, mustard, lemon juice, anchovies, black garlic, chopped garlic, pepper, and salt in a blender. Pulse several times, then, with the blender running, drizzle in the olive oil through the hole in the lid and blend until the dressing is creamy and smooth.

Make the Parmesan crumbs

Preheat the oven to 350°F. Line a small baking sheet with parchment paper (or a silicone baking mat, if you have one) and spritz with nonstick cooking spray. Put the Parmesan in the center of the prepared baking sheet and use your hands to spread it out into a thin layer. Crank plenty of pepper over the cheese, then bake, rotating the pan once halfway through, until the Parmesan fuses into a single sheet (like a giant cheese cracker) and turns golden brown, 10 to 12 minutes.

Remove the pan from the oven and let the cheese cool completely, then break it up into shards with your hands.

Make the salad

Bring a medium saucepan of water to a simmer over medium-high heat and add the vinegar. One at a time, crack the eggs into a small, shallow bowl and gently slide them into the water. Cook the eggs, adjusting the heat to maintain a gentle simmer, until the whites are set but the yolks are still runny, about 3 minutes. Scoop the poached eggs out of the water with a slotted spoon and slide them onto a paper towel to drain. Season lightly with salt.

Combine the greens, dressing (give it a quick whisk if it has separated), and half the Parmesan crumbs in a large bowl, toss well, and transfer to serving bowls. Top each with a poached egg, a drizzle of olive oil, and a sprinkle of flaky salt. Sprinkle on the remaining Parmesan crumbs and serve.

MUSHROOMS

Fabulous Fungus

Mushroom–Green Peppercorn Gravy for Biscuits

There's a swordfish dish at Playa Provisions in which the sauce practically steals the show. Because the fish is so meaty, we merge a classic marsala with the kind of creamy, green peppercorn–spiked sauce you'd see on steak at a French bistro. The result eats like a gravy, so substantial and luxurious—though the marsala and peppercorns keep the richness in check—that at home I often use it to make a full-on dinner from whatever mushrooms catch my eye at the market. It's fantastic on fish, meat, and polenta, sure, but I'm a big fan of spooning it over biscuits, fresh from the oven.

SERVES 4 TO 6

4 to 6 Buttermilk Biscuits (recipe follows), warm
2 tablespoons extra-virgin olive oil
1 yellow onion, diced
3 garlic cloves, minced
1 pound cremini mushrooms, sliced
2½ teaspoons kosher salt, plus more if needed
½ teaspoon freshly ground black pepper, plus more as needed
½ teaspoon fresh rosemary
1 tablespoon porcini mushroom powder
1 tablespoon drained green peppercorns in brine
1 tablespoon all-purpose flour
½ cup sweet marsala wine
1½ cups unsalted chicken stock
½ cup heavy cream
Small handful of parsley, chopped

Make the biscuits as directed on page 145. While they bake, heat the olive oil in a large saucepan over medium until it shimmers. Add the onion and garlic and cook, stirring occasionally, until they begin to brown, about 5 minutes.

Add the mushrooms, 1½ teaspoons of the salt, and a few cranks of pepper and raise the heat to medium-high. Cook, stirring occasionally, until the mushrooms are lightly browned, 6 to 8 minutes. Stir in the rosemary, porcini powder, and green peppercorns, then stir in the flour.

Add the marsala and stir, scraping up all the browned bits from the bottom of the pan with a wooden spoon, then cook until the wine has more or less fully evaporated. Add the stock and bring to a simmer, then reduce the heat to maintain a gentle simmer and cook until thick enough to coat the back of a spoon, 6 to 8 minutes.

Add the cream and simmer until the sauce thickens slightly and looks exactly like the kind of gravy you'd want to pour all over a freshly baked biscuit, 2 to 3 minutes more. Stir in the remaining 1 teaspoon salt (or more to taste), plenty of pepper, and the parsley.

Spoon the gravy generously over the warm biscuits and serve.

(continued)

Buttermilk Biscuits

I'm someone who likes to be prepared. Before the Seattle season of *Top Chef*, for example, I bought myself a geoduck, an enormous clam native to the Pacific Northwest, just in case it factored into a challenge. How else would I know how to peel its elephant-trunk-like siphon? So when I heard I'd be competing in Charleston for my second time on the show, I knew I'd be in trouble if I didn't have a biscuit recipe dialed in. I was right, and the biscuits won me a Quickfire Challenge. Because I've been fine-tuning them ever since, these incredibly fluffy, flaky biscuits are even better.

When you handle the dough, be sure to use a light touch—the less you work it, the better the biscuits. And take the time to fully freeze the dough before baking. Not only does this mean you'll always have biscuits in your back pocket, but when they go straight from freezer to oven, the center stays super moist and they toast up to a beautiful golden brown.

MAKES 12

4¼ cups all-purpose flour, plus more for dusting
2 tablespoons baking powder
1 tablespoon kosher salt
1 tablespoon sugar
1½ sticks (12 tablespoons) cold unsalted butter, cut into small cubes
1½ cups heavy cream, plus more for brushing
⅔ cup buttermilk
Flaky sea salt, like Maldon

(continued)

Combine the flour, baking powder, salt, and sugar in a large bowl. Add the butter and use your fingertips to mix and smoosh each piece of butter into the flour mixture just until it's evenly distributed. Add the cream and buttermilk and mix gently with your hands just until you have a shaggy dough that doesn't quite come together into a cohesive blob.

Dump the dough onto a lightly floured work surface and pat it into a rough rectangle that's about 8 by 10 inches. Fold the dough in thirds like a letter: Fold one of the short sides up to cover the middle third of the dough, then fold the other short side down. Use a lightly floured rolling pin to roll the dough into a rectangle that's 1½ to 2 inches thick.

Using a round cutter, the rim of a drinking glass, or just a knife, cut the dough into 12 biscuits roughly 2¾ inches in diameter (you'll end up making the last few biscuits from the scraps—just handle the dough as little and as gently as you can). Put the biscuits on a baking sheet and freeze until fully frozen. Transfer them to a container or freezer bag and keep them in the freezer until you're ready to bake them, up to 3 months.

When you're ready to bake, preheat the oven to 375°F with a rack in the center position.

Put the frozen biscuits (as many as you want to make at a time) on a baking sheet with a little space between each one. Brush the tops with a little cream and sprinkle lightly with flaky salt. Bake on the center rack, rotating the pan halfway through, until the biscuits are just golden brown on top, 25 to 30 minutes. Serve warm.

Ginger-Glazed King Oyster Mushrooms with Green Bean Dressing

King oyster mushrooms, also known as king trumpets, have large, thick stems with an almost meaty chew and juicy texture. I sear them to a gorgeous golden brown, like I would chicken thighs or pork chops, then hit them with a syrupy miso-ginger glaze. Just before serving, I spoon on a dressing that adds both acidity and a little textural variation—what might look like sliced chives are actually green beans—for a crisp crunch.

For the dressing

Kosher salt
10 haricots verts
2 tablespoons unseasoned rice vinegar
1 tablespoon fish sauce
1 tablespoon honey
1 tablespoon extra-virgin olive oil
1 teaspoon grated fresh ginger
1 teaspoon toasted sesame oil
½ teaspoon gochugaru (Korean chile flakes) or crushed Calabrian chile
Finely grated zest and juice of 1 lime
Large pinch of thinly sliced fresh chives
1 garlic clove, grated on a Microplane

For the mushrooms

2 tablespoons soy sauce
2 tablespoons sake
2 tablespoons mirin
2 tablespoons shiro (white) miso paste
2 tablespoons sugar
1 tablespoon grated fresh ginger
2 garlic cloves, grated on a Microplane
Freshly ground black pepper
2 tablespoons neutral oil, like canola
1½ pounds king oyster mushrooms, bottom ⅛ inch or so trimmed, halved lengthwise

Make the dressing

Bring a small saucepan of water to a boil and salt it generously. Add the haricots verts and cook just until bright green, about 30 seconds. Drain and run under cold water, pat dry, and thinly slice.

Just before serving, whisk together the vinegar, fish sauce, honey, olive oil, ginger, sesame oil, gochugaru, lime zest, lime juice, chives, garlic, and ¼ teaspoon salt in a medium bowl, then stir in the haricots verts.

Cook the mushrooms

Whisk together the soy sauce, sake, mirin, miso, sugar, ginger, garlic, and pepper to taste in a small bowl and set aside.

Heat 1 tablespoon of the oil in a large heavy skillet over medium-high heat until it shimmers. Add half the mushrooms to the skillet, cut-side down, and cook, without stirring but gently pressing down on them with a spatula to encourage even browning, until golden brown on the bottom, 3 to 4 minutes. Transfer the mushrooms to a plate, add the remaining 1 tablespoon oil to the pan, and brown the second batch of mushrooms.

Return all the mushrooms to the pan, browned-side up. Pour the glaze over the mushrooms and cook over medium-high heat, flipping the mushrooms once or twice, until the liquid thickens into a syrupy glaze, 3 to 4 minutes. Take the pan off the heat and let the mushrooms sit until the glaze cools and thickens slightly, about 3 minutes.

Transfer the mushrooms to a serving platter, cut-side up, and drizzle on any glaze left in the pan. Give the dressing a quick whisk, then spoon it on and serve.

Al Pastor Maitake Tacos with Cabbage Slaw

Like king oyster mushrooms, maitake (or hen of the woods) mushrooms can almost convince you they're meat. Especially here, where they're coated in a sauce that evokes al pastor—Mexican marinated pork cooked on vertical spits with chunks of pineapple—and roasted until they're crisp at the edges. At the restaurant, we serve them as the centerpiece of a composed dish. At home, though, they belong in tacos, with creamy slices of avocado and this crunchy, bright purple slaw.

SERVES 4 TO 6

For the slaw

¼ cup lime juice (2 to 3 limes)
2 tablespoons pineapple juice
2 tablespoons honey
1 teaspoon kosher salt
½ teaspoon freshly ground black pepper
¼ cup thinly sliced red onion
1 Fresno chile, seeded and thinly sliced
3 cups very thinly sliced red cabbage (a mandoline helps)
Handful of cilantro, coarsely chopped

For the mushrooms

1 pound maitake (aka hen of the woods) mushrooms
⅓ cup pineapple juice
¼ cup neutral oil, like canola
4 tablespoons (2 ounces) achiote paste
2 tablespoons apple cider vinegar
2 tablespoons light brown sugar
1 tablespoon soy sauce
1 teaspoon dried oregano
1 teaspoon ground cumin
1 teaspoon chili powder
1 teaspoon kosher salt, plus more as needed
4 garlic cloves, peeled
1 canned chipotle pepper in adobo sauce, plus 2 tablespoons of the adobo

For serving

12 (4- to 5-inch) flour or corn tortillas
2 tablespoons avocado oil or vegetable oil
1 large Hass avocado, pitted, peeled, and sliced

(continued)

Make the slaw

Whisk together the lime juice, pineapple juice, honey, salt, and pepper in a large bowl. Add the onion and chile and let marinate for 2 to 3 minutes. Add the cabbage and cilantro and toss well. Set aside to marinate while you make the mushrooms.

Roast the mushrooms and serve

Preheat the oven to 375°F. Line a large baking sheet with parchment paper (or a silicone baking mat, if you have one). Trim the base of the mushrooms, then pull them apart into large clusters, each about the size of a large floret of broccoli, keeping the base intact so the clusters hold together. Spread the mushrooms over the prepared baking sheet.

Combine the pineapple juice, oil, achiote paste, vinegar, brown sugar, soy sauce, oregano, cumin, chili powder, salt, garlic, chipotle, and adobo in a blender and blend until smooth. Pour the mixture over the mushrooms and toss, rubbing gently so they're smothered and all the nooks are coated. Season with a little more salt. Roast, rotating the pan halfway through, until the mushrooms are crisp at the edges, 25 to 30 minutes. Keep warm.

Rub both sides of the tortillas with a little oil. Toast the tortillas a few at a time in a hot pan, flipping once, until they're hot and pliable, about 20 seconds per side. As they're done, wrap them in a kitchen towel to keep warm.

Serve the warm tortillas, mushrooms, slaw, and avocado family-style and have everyone make their own tacos.

Mushroom Bolognese

When Nick, Hudson, and I arrived in Bologna, Italy, for a cycling trip, we were jet-lagged zombies. Loopy and ravenous, we put our bags down at our hotel and lumbered to the restaurant on the corner. I told Hudson that Bolognese was from Bologna, so he should probably get the tagliatelle. He did, and at first bite, his drooping eyelids popped open, and he finished the whole bowl in about a minute. For the next eight days, he ate Bolognese at least once a day.

When we came home, he sighed and announced, "I'm really going to miss Bolognese." So I set to work on my Bolognese game. Even though Hudson's a great eater, I couldn't resist doing the mom thing and adding mushrooms to get some more vegetables in there. Then I realized I loved it that way, so nowadays I use loads of cremini mushrooms and a little dried porcini for an umami-packed sauce. (A few shakes of Sabatino truffle zest, a sneaky pantry trick, doesn't hurt, either, to really drill in that big flavor.) Just one pork sausage link, for the texture and flavor, is all the meat you need. Hudson eats the Bolognese just as greedily.

SERVES 4

For the Bolognese

1 ounce dried porcini mushrooms
2 tablespoons extra-virgin olive oil, plus more for garnish
4 ounces sweet Italian sausage, casings removed
1 small yellow onion, diced
1 medium carrot, diced
1 celery stalk, diced
6 garlic cloves, minced
1 pound cremini mushrooms, trimmed and pulsed in a food processor until finely chopped
½ cup tomato paste
1 teaspoon balsamic vinegar
½ teaspoon light brown sugar
Large pinch of chopped thyme leaves
Pinch of red chile flakes
¼ cup dry red wine
2 dried bay leaves
1½ cups low-sodium mushroom broth
1 teaspoon anchovy juice or anchovy paste
2½ teaspoons kosher salt, plus more as needed
½ teaspoon freshly ground black pepper
¼ cup heavy cream

For the pasta

Kosher salt
1 pound rigatoni, cavatelli, or your favorite pasta shape
Large handful of basil leaves, torn at the last minute
¼ cup finely grated Parmesan cheese, plus more for serving

(continued)

Make the Bolognese

Soak the porcini in ½ cup hot water in a small bowl for 30 minutes. Drain the porcini, reserving the soaking liquid, and coarsely chop.

Heat the olive oil in a large saucepan or Dutch oven over medium heat until it shimmers. Add the sausage and cook, breaking it apart into little bits with a spoon or potato masher, until it browns and crisps into toasty little crumbs, 6 to 8 minutes.

Add the onion, carrot, celery, and garlic and cook, stirring occasionally and scraping the pan to dislodge any browned bits, until the vegetables soften and begin to brown, 5 to 7 minutes. Add the cremini mushrooms, raise the heat to high, and cook, stirring occasionally, until almost all of the liquid the mushrooms release has evaporated, 6 minutes or so more.

Add the tomato paste, soaked porcini mushrooms, vinegar, brown sugar, thyme, and chile flakes. Cook, stirring, for a couple of minutes, then add the wine and bay leaves and stir, scraping up any browned bits from the bottom of the pan.

Add the reserved porcini soaking liquid, the mushroom broth, and anchovy juice and season with 2½ teaspoons salt and ½ teaspoon pepper. Bring to a simmer, then reduce the heat to maintain a moderate simmer and cook, stirring occasionally, until the liquid reduces and the sauce thickens to a slightly saucy ragù, about 20 minutes.

Add the cream and simmer for 5 minutes to thicken the sauce once more. Stir in the basil, Parmesan, and more salt to taste. Keep warm off the heat while you cook the pasta. (Or let the Bolognese cool and store in an airtight container in the refrigerator for up to 3 days. Reheat before serving.)

Make the pasta

Bring a large pot of water to a boil and salt it generously. Add the pasta and cook according to the package instructions, stirring occasionally, until al dente. Drain the pasta, reserving about 1 cup of the pasta water.

Add the pasta to the Bolognese sauce along with ½ cup of the reserved pasta water. Cook over high heat, stirring vigorously and gradually adding more pasta water if necessary to loosen the sauce, until the pasta is well coated, about 30 seconds. Season to taste with salt.

Serve sprinkled with more Parmesan.

Very Mushroom-Barley Soup with Leeks and Gruyère

When I ate mushroom barley soup as a kid—either at Jewish delis or at home from a Campbell's can—the bowls were always more about the barley than the mushrooms. And that was fine with me, because even as a kid I loved barley. The chew, the way it quietly popped between your teeth, the toasty nuttiness. It's one of those grains that's good for you but doesn't necessarily taste like it is. The version I cook nowadays has enough barley to make each bowl a meal, but it's more mushroom focused, a great place to showcase flavorful varieties like shiitake and oyster, along with some porcini powder (one of my secret pantry weapons) to bump up the umami. Caramelized leeks add their sophisticated flavor and little cubes of Gruyère stirred in at the last minute contribute gooey fun.

SERVES 4 TO 6

3 tablespoons extra-virgin olive oil, plus more for serving
1 large leek, white and pale green parts only, halved lengthwise, cleaned, and thinly sliced
1 teaspoon light brown sugar
3 teaspoons kosher salt, plus more as needed
1½ pounds mixed mushrooms (like button, oyster, and stemmed shiitake), sliced
2 celery stalks, diced
1 large carrot, diced
1 medium yellow onion, diced
4 garlic cloves, minced
3 tablespoons tomato paste
1 tablespoon soy sauce
2 teaspoons porcini mushroom powder
1 teaspoon ground coriander
1 teaspoon smoked paprika
6 cups unsalted beef stock (chicken or vegetable is okay, too)
½ cup uncooked pearled barley
Handful of flat-leaf parsley, chopped
½ teaspoon freshly ground black pepper
4 ounces Gruyère cheese, cut into ½-inch cubes

Heat 2 tablespoons of the olive oil in a medium pot or Dutch oven over medium-high heat until it shimmers. Add the leeks, brown sugar, and ½ teaspoon of the salt. Cook, stirring almost constantly, until the leeks begin to brown, about 5 minutes. Add the mushrooms and ½ teaspoon of the remaining salt and cook, stirring occasionally, until the mushrooms begin to brown and soften, 5 to 10 minutes. Transfer half of the mushroom and leek mixture to a bowl and set aside.

Add the remaining 1 tablespoon oil to the pan along with the celery, carrot, onion, and garlic. Cook, stirring occasionally, for 5 minutes or so, then add the tomato paste, soy sauce, porcini powder, coriander, and smoked paprika. Cook, stirring and scraping the pan constantly so nothing burns, for 2 minutes.

Add the stock, barley, and remaining 2 teaspoons salt and bring to a boil. Reduce the heat to maintain a moderate simmer, cover, and cook until the barley is fully tender but still retains a slight bite, about 30 minutes.

Return the mushrooms and leeks to the pan and simmer just until they're warmed through, a couple minutes. Season with salt to taste, then stir in the parsley and pepper and ladle the soup into bowls.

Add the Gruyère to the bowls and give it a minute or two to become melty and gooey. Drizzle with a little more olive oil and serve.

Roasted Button Mushrooms with Thyme, Vinegar, and Black Garlic

With a little care, you can turn even the most ordinary of mushrooms into a thrill. The key is letting them cook, undisturbed, so they have time to develop some deep caramelization without the juices inside escaping. This leaves the mushrooms luscious and nearly bursting with concentrated mushroom flavor. Black garlic doubles down on all that dark umami richness and a splash of vinegar brings a touch of balance and brightness.

SERVES 4

2 black garlic cloves, peeled
1 tablespoon extra-virgin olive oil
1 heaping teaspoon kosher salt
½ stick (4 tablespoons) unsalted butter, melted
2 garlic cloves, minced
Large pinch of chopped fresh thyme, plus more leaves for garnish
¼ teaspoon freshly ground black pepper
1½ pounds button or cremini mushrooms, trimmed
1½ tablespoons sherry vinegar

Preheat the oven to 450°F.

Mash the black garlic, olive oil, and salt to a paste in a large bowl. Add the melted butter, minced garlic, thyme, and pepper and stir to combine. Add the mushrooms, toss to coat, and spread them in an even layer on a large baking sheet.

Roast, undisturbed, until tender and nicely browned, about 25 minutes. Remove the pan from the oven, drizzle on the vinegar, stir well, and roast for 5 minutes more, just to let the added moisture evaporate. Garnish with more thyme and serve hot.

Shiitake-Chestnut Holiday Rice

Nick's mom loved to cook Thanksgiving dinner, and we loved to help. But when she got sick, we offered to take on the task. One of her favorite foods was chestnuts, so along with the yams and stuffing and turkey, I made this rice, and it was such a hit that I've made it every year since.

I've always loved chestnuts in Asian contexts, so I look to chewy shiitake along with sesame oil, soy sauce, and oyster sauce to support the fall flavor provided by those sweet, starchy (and conveniently precooked and vacuum-packed) nuts. After a quick sauté of aromatics, it all goes into the rice cooker along with mushroom stock, so it cooks up to glossy perfection every time. And like stuffing and other Thanksgiving staples, it's just as craveable the next day.

SERVES 4 TO 6

2 cups short-grain white rice (like sushi rice)
2 tablespoons toasted sesame oil
2 tablespoons unsalted butter
1 large shallot, minced
1 teaspoon minced fresh ginger
8 ounces fresh shiitake mushrooms, stemmed and sliced
2 teaspoons kosher salt
¼ cup mirin
3 tablespoons oyster sauce
½ cup roasted peeled chestnuts, coarsely chopped
1½ cups unsalted mushroom stock or water
3 tablespoons soy sauce
Handful of thinly sliced scallions, for garnish
Fried shallots, store-bought or homemade (page 31), for garnish

Put the rice in a bowl and rinse with cold water, pouring off the water and refilling the bowl until the water is clear when you stir. Drain the rice and set aside.

Heat the sesame oil and butter in a large skillet over medium-low until the butter melts. Add the shallot and ginger and cook, stirring occasionally, until they are soft and translucent but not browned, 4 to 5 minutes.

Add the mushrooms, sprinkle with 1 teaspoon of the salt, and cook, stirring occasionally, until softened, about 2 minutes. Turn off the heat and stir in the mirin, oyster sauce, and chestnuts.

Combine the rinsed rice, mushroom-chestnut mixture, stock, remaining 1 teaspoon salt, and soy sauce in a rice cooker and stir to combine. Set the rice cooker to the white rice setting, and forget about it.

When the rice is done, give it a thorough but gentle stir to mix in the mushrooms and chestnuts, which will have risen to the top. Transfer to a serving bowl, garnish with the scallions and fried shallots, and serve.

FLOWERING HEADS

Broccoli, Brussels, and Buds

My Favorite Stuffed Cabbage with Chili-Garlic Sauce and Cashew Relish

To bring cabbage from side to center of the table, I make these special cabbage rolls filled with a textural playground, the silky cabbage leaves enrobing creamy sweet potato and hearty lentils, crunchy bits of cashew and chewy bits of bacon, all seasoned with warm South Asian spices. They're enlivened by a garlicky, sweet-tart sauce made from piquillo peppers and Kashmiri chili powder and topped with a crunchy cashew relish. It's dinner in a very pretty package.

SERVES 4 TO 6

For the sweet potatoes and cabbage

2 medium sweet potatoes (about 1¾ pounds total)
Kosher salt
1 large head savoy cabbage

For the rolls

4 slices bacon, chopped
2 tablespoons extra-virgin olive oil
1 medium shallot, minced
1 teaspoon minced fresh ginger
1 teaspoon black mustard seeds
2 garlic cloves, minced
½ teaspoon curry powder, like Madras
½ teaspoon ground turmeric
1 cup cooked black lentils
¼ cup chopped unsalted roasted cashews
Small handful of cilantro, chopped
2 scallions, sliced
1 teaspoon kosher salt
½ teaspoon freshly ground black pepper
2 tablespoons butter, at room temperature
½ cup unsalted chicken stock
About ¾ cup Red Chili Garlic Sauce (recipe follows)

For the cashew relish

¼ cup coarsely chopped unsalted roasted cashews
Small handful of cilantro, chopped
2 scallions, sliced
1 medium garlic clove, minced
Finely grated zest and juice of 1 lime
1 tablespoon toasted sesame seeds
1 tablespoon extra-virgin olive oil
½ teaspoon kosher salt
⅛ teaspoon freshly ground black pepper

(continued)

Prep the sweet potatoes and cabbage

Preheat the oven to 400°F.

Poke holes all over the sweet potatoes with a fork, put them on a baking sheet, and bake just until they're fully tender, about 1 hour. Remove them from the oven and let cool (keep the oven on), then peel them and cut them into ¼-inch pieces. Set aside.

While the sweet potatoes roast, bring a large pot of water to a boil and add a handful of salt. Line a baking sheet with paper towels. Remove and discard the blemished outer leaves of the cabbage and cut off the base. Separate 8 intact large leaves from the heat and make an upside-down V cut to remove the thick stem portion of each leaf. (Reserve the rest of the cabbage for another use.)

Cook the cabbage leaves in the boiling water just until they're pliable enough to fold without breaking, a minute or two. Drain the leaves on the prepared baking sheet and let them cool.

Make the rolls

Cook the bacon in a large skillet over medium heat until crisp. Transfer it to a bowl with a slotted spoon, leaving the fat behind.

Add the olive oil to the pan, then add the shallot, ginger, and mustard seeds and cook, stirring occasionally, until the shallot and ginger are light golden, 6 to 8 minutes. Add the garlic, curry powder, and turmeric and cook until the garlic is fragrant and light golden, about 1 minute more.

Add the roasted sweet potatoes, lentils, cooked bacon, and cashews and toss to coat everything in the fragrant fat. Fold in the cilantro and scallions and season with the salt and pepper. Remove the pan from the heat and let the mixture sit until it's cool enough to handle.

Trim any thick stems from the back of the blanched cabbage leaves. One at a time, lay the cabbage leaves concave side up on a clean work surface and add about ⅓ cup of the filling (or a little more for the largest leaves) near the base of the stem. Roll up each leaf like a burrito (roll, tuck in the sides, roll). If your leaves are small, double them up.

Melt the butter in a large oven-safe skillet (I like cast iron here) over low heat, swirling it around to coat the bottom and sides of the pan as it melts. Add the stuffed cabbage leaves seam-side down, increase the heat to medium, and let them sizzle for 6 minutes, just to get some caramelization starting. Pour the stock over the cabbage rolls and season them lightly with salt.

Transfer the skillet to the oven and bake, basting the rolls halfway through, until the stock has mostly reduced, 20 to 25 minutes. Spoon the red chili garlic sauce over the cabbage rolls and bake for 4 minutes more.

Make the cashew relish and serve

Stir together all the relish ingredients in a small bowl.

Remove the pan from the oven, spoon the cashew relish over the top of the rolls, and serve.

Red Chili Garlic Sauce

MAKES ABOUT 1 CUP

1 (8-ounce) jar roasted piquillo peppers, drained
10 cloves Garlic Confit (page 119) or 2 raw cloves, plus ¼ cup confit oil or olive oil
1 medium garlic clove, peeled
1 tablespoon sherry vinegar
1 tablespoon honey
1 teaspoon Kashmiri chili powder, or 1 scant teaspoon cayenne pepper
1 teaspoon kosher salt
⅛ teaspoon freshly ground black pepper

Combine all the ingredients in a blender and blend until smooth. The sauce will keep in an airtight container in the fridge for up to 1 week.

Roasted Romanesco with Boquerones, Harissa Breadcrumbs, and Creamy Mustard Dressing

I'll admit that the first time I bought romanesco, with its whorled florets the color of broccoli stems, I wanted to look at it as much as I wanted to cook it. Yet while the otherworldly brassica seems alien, it's easy to find and contributes more than just its looks. Like cauliflower with more structure, romanesco has a fantastic texture that can stand up to a hard roast without losing its bite. Its flavor is mild, so I go big with a mustardy dressing, crunchy breadcrumbs charged with harissa, and boquerones (Spanish vinegar-marinated anchovies), which lend a bold, briny acidity and which I'll find just about any excuse to use.

SERVES 4 TO 6

For the creamy mustard dressing

3 tablespoons extra-virgin olive oil
2 tablespoons red wine vinegar
2 tablespoons crème fraîche
2 garlic cloves, grated on a Microplane
1 teaspoon Dijon mustard
1 teaspoon whole-grain mustard
Pinch of chopped fresh dill
½ teaspoon kosher salt
¼ teaspoon freshly ground black pepper

For the romanesco

2 medium heads romanesco (about 1 pound each), cut into medium florets
3 tablespoons extra-virgin olive oil
1 teaspoon kosher salt
½ teaspoon freshly ground black pepper
8 drained marinated white anchovy fillets (boquerones), sliced lengthwise into thirds
½ cup Harissa Breadcrumbs (recipe follows), or more to taste
Chopped fresh dill, for serving

Make the dressing

Whisk together all the dressing ingredients in a medium bowl.

Roast the romanesco

Preheat the oven to 400°F.

Put the romanesco florets on a large baking sheet, drizzle with the olive oil, season with the salt and pepper, and toss to coat. Roast, tossing the florets and rotating the baking sheet once halfway through, until the romanesco is tender and the edges are a deep roasty color, 18 to 20 minutes.

Transfer the romanesco to a serving platter and top with the anchovies. Give the dressing a quick whisk, then drizzle it on, garnish with the breadcrumbs and some dill, and serve.

(continued)

Harissa Breadcrumbs

MAKES 1 CUP

1½ cups crustless cubes good country bread
3 tablespoons neutral oil, like canola
2 garlic cloves, minced
2 teaspoons harissa
½ teaspoon kosher salt
A couple pinches of freshly ground black pepper

Preheat the oven to 350°F.

Pulse the bread in a food processor until broken down into coarse crumbs, stopping to stir between pulses if necessary. Transfer to a medium bowl.

Whisk together the oil, garlic, and harissa in a small bowl. Pour the oil mixture over the breadcrumbs, season with the salt and pepper, and toss to coat.

Spread the breadcrumbs in an even layer over a small baking sheet and bake, stirring halfway through, until golden and crisp, 12 to 15 minutes. Transfer the crumbs to a paper towel–lined plate to drain and cool.

The breadcrumbs will keep in an airtight container (with a folded paper towel at the bottom to soak up any extra moisture or oil) at room temp for a day or two.

Broccoli-Potato Salad with Curry and Jammy Beet-Pickled Eggs

Hudson has been a broccoli guy since preschool, so at my house we eat a lot of it. So much so that it ends up in places you might not think it belongs. Here crunchy florets star in what is essentially potato salad, the picnic classic souped up with a particularly vibrant dressing, a touch of curry powder, and these eye-catching quick-pickled eggs with jammy yolks. Those eggs hang out briefly in brine, just long enough to pick up some acidity and the bright pink color from beet juice without losing the tenderness of the whites.

SERVES 4

For the dressing

3 tablespoons apple cider vinegar
3 tablespoons extra-virgin olive oil
2 tablespoons sour cream
2 tablespoons mayonnaise
2 teaspoons Dijon mustard
1 teaspoon honey
1 teaspoon Madras curry powder
2 garlic cloves, grated on a Microplane
Big pinch of chopped fresh dill
1 teaspoon kosher salt
¼ teaspoon freshly ground black pepper
1 medium shallot, minced

For the salad

12 ounces fingerling potatoes (assorted colors, if you can find them)
Kosher salt
1 medium head broccoli (about 1 pound), cut into medium florets
½ cup finely diced celery
4 Pickled Jammy Eggs (recipe follows)
Freshly ground black pepper
1 teaspoon flaky sea salt, like Maldon

Make the dressing

Whisk together all the dressing ingredients in a medium bowl and set aside.

Make the salad

Put the potatoes in a medium saucepan, add water to cover by about an inch, and salt the water generously. Bring to a boil, then reduce the heat to maintain a simmer and cook until you can easily pierce the potatoes with a sharp knife, about 15 minutes. Scoop out the potatoes and set them aside to cool. Keep the water boiling.

Fill a large bowl with ice and water. Add the broccoli to the boiling water and cook until just tender (you still want some bite), 3 to 4 minutes. Transfer the broccoli to the ice water and let it cool completely. Drain well.

Cut the broccoli into bite-size pieces and thinly slice any thick stems, then transfer to a large bowl. Slice the potatoes into ½-inch-thick rounds and add them to the bowl with the broccoli. Add the dressing (give it a quick whisk if it has separated) and celery, toss to coat, and season with salt and pepper to taste. Transfer to a serving platter.

Quarter the eggs lengthwise (wipe your knife between each cut for a clean look) and sprinkle them with some flaky salt and pepper. Serve the salad with the eggs on top.

(continued)

Pickled Jammy Eggs

MAKES 4

1 cup apple cider vinegar
½ cup beet juice
2 tablespoons sugar
1 tablespoon kosher salt
½ teaspoon baking soda
4 large eggs

Combine the vinegar, beet juice, sugar, and salt in a small saucepan. Cook over medium heat, whisking constantly until the salt and sugar have fully dissolved. Remove from the heat and let cool to room temperature.

Bring a medium saucepan of water to a boil. Fill a large bowl with ice and water. Stir the baking soda into the boiling water (this helps the eggs peel neatly later) and carefully add the eggs. Set a timer for 8 minutes. After 8 minutes, carefully transfer the eggs to the ice water and let them hang out for 5 minutes.

Carefully peel the eggs and put them in a large resealable bag. Carefully pour in the pickling liquid and seal the bag, gently forcing out as much air as you can. Put the bag in a bowl, in case it leaks, and refrigerate for at least 25 minutes but no more than 1 hour.

Drain the eggs and transfer to an airtight container. The eggs will keep in the fridge for up to 2 days.

Crispy Smashed Brussels Sprouts with Golden Raisins, Mustard Seeds, and Bagna Cauda

Brussels sprouts have gone through a couple of phases. Back in the day, they were boiled to mush and earned themselves some devoted haters. In the past decade or two, their rep has been resurrected by the cooks who roasted (and chefs who deep-fried) the sturdy sprouts to accentuate their sweetness and preserve their interior crunch. Well, I'm hoping to introduce phase three. Because there's something luscious and lovely about a fully cooked sprout: the silky texture and its ability to soak up flavor, as it does here with a buttery anchovy-fueled sauce that calls to mind bagna cauda, with pickled mustard seeds and raisins chiming in for balance. The magic comes when you flatten the vegetable, creating edges that get crispy in the oven.

SERVES 4

For the raisins

2 tablespoons sherry vinegar
1 tablespoon honey
2 teaspoons yellow mustard seeds
½ teaspoon kosher salt
¼ cup golden raisins

For the bagna cauda

½ stick (4 tablespoons) unsalted butter
¼ cup extra-virgin olive oil
8 oil-packed anchovy fillets, drained and chopped
4 garlic cloves, minced

For the Brussels sprouts

Kosher salt
1½ pounds Brussels sprouts, bottoms trimmed and blemished leaves removed
¼ teaspoon freshly ground black pepper
Big pinch of finely chopped parsley

(continued)

Make the raisins

Combine the vinegar, honey, mustard seeds, salt, and 2 tablespoons water in a small saucepan and bring to a simmer over high heat. Reduce the heat to maintain a gentle simmer and cook for 4 minutes, so the mustard seeds can cook and some of the liquid evaporates.

Put the raisins in a small heatproof bowl, pour in the vinegar mixture, and set aside until the raisins soak up the liquid, at least 15 minutes.

Make the bagna cauda

Wipe out the saucepan you used for the vinegar mixture, then add the butter, olive oil, anchovies, and garlic and set the pan over low heat. Cook at a low bubble (the butter will separate, but that's totally fine) just until the garlic turns a light golden color, 3 to 4 minutes. Remove from the heat.

Make the Brussels sprouts

Preheat the oven to 425°F.

Bring a medium pot of water to a boil and add about ¼ cup salt. Add the Brussels sprouts and boil until a small sharp knife goes in easily, 8 to 9 minutes. Drain them well, transfer them to a large baking sheet, and pat them dry with a kitchen towel (you want them to be as dry as possible).

Working on a cutting board, use the bottom of a plate, bowl, or mason jar to firmly press down on each Brussels sprout to flatten slightly, trying your best to keep them in one piece. Put them in a large bowl, sprinkle on 1 teaspoon salt and pepper to taste, then spoon in about half the butter mixture, avoiding the chunks of garlic and anchovy at the bottom of the pan. Toss gently to coat.

Line a large baking sheet with parchment paper (or a silicone baking mat, if you have one). Spread the Brussels sprouts on the prepared baking sheet and roast, flipping once halfway through, until golden brown all over and crispy at the edges, 35 to 40 minutes.

Just before serving, warm the remaining butter mixture over low heat. Turn off the heat and stir in the raisin mixture and parsley. Serve the Brussels sprouts on a platter, topped with the butter mixture.

Cauliflower with Spiced Tomato, Garlic Tahini, and Pine Nut Dukkah

Cauliflower is one of the few vegetables given frequent main-event treatment—I'm thinking whole roasted heads and cauliflower steaks. When I'm looking to treat cauliflower as dinner's headliner, I often look to regular old florets, which brown so beautifully in a hot oven. Then I use the other elements of the dish to make the meal feel special and complete, tossing that sweet, slightly nutty cauliflower in spiced tomato sauciness, adding richness with a creamy, garlicky tahini drizzle, and sprinkling on a crunchy mixture of spices, sesame seeds, and pine nuts inspired by Egyptian dukkah.

SERVES 4

For the tahini sauce

10 cloves Garlic Confit (page 119) or 2 raw cloves, plus 3 tablespoons confit oil or olive oil
3 tablespoons well-stirred tahini
Juice of 1 lemon
½ teaspoon kosher salt

For the dukkah

1 tablespoon coriander seeds
1 heaping teaspoon cumin seeds
¼ cup coarsely chopped toasted pine nuts
1 heaping tablespoon toasted white sesame seeds
1 heaping tablespoon toasted black sesame seeds
½ teaspoon kosher salt
½ teaspoon freshly ground black pepper
½ teaspoon sugar

For the cauliflower

1 large head cauliflower, trimmed and cut into medium florets (about 7 cups)
6 tablespoons extra-virgin olive oil
Kosher salt and freshly ground black pepper
1 small fennel bulb (about 6 ounces), diced
1 medium yellow onion, diced
2 garlic cloves, minced
1 tablespoon harissa
½ cup dry white wine
¾ cup crushed canned tomatoes
½ cup sliced drained roasted red peppers
2 teaspoons ground coriander
1 teaspoon ground turmeric
Small handful of mixed fresh herbs, like cilantro, basil, and parsley, chopped

(continued)

Make the tahini sauce

Combine all the sauce ingredients along with 2 tablespoons water in a blender and blend until smooth, gradually adding more water if necessary for a thick but drizzle-able consistency. Set aside.

Make the dukkah

Combine the coriander and cumin seeds in a small skillet and toast over medium heat, stirring frequently, until fragrant, 1 to 2 minutes. Finely grind them with a mortar and pestle or a spice grinder and transfer to a small bowl. Add the pine nuts, white and black sesame seeds, salt, black pepper, and sugar and stir well. Set aside.

Make the cauliflower

Preheat the oven to 400°F.

Toss the cauliflower on a large baking sheet with 3 tablespoons of the olive oil, 1 tablespoon salt, and 1 teaspoon black pepper. Spread the florets into a single layer and roast, tossing once, until lightly browned and tender but with a slight bite, 20 to 25 minutes. Let cool.

Meanwhile, heat the remaining 3 tablespoons olive oil in a Dutch oven or large heavy-bottomed skillet over medium-high heat until it shimmers. Add the fennel, onion, and garlic and cook, stirring occasionally, until the vegetables are softened and golden brown, about 6 minutes. Stir in the harissa and cook until it darkens a bit and begins to dry out, 1 to 2 minutes.

Add the wine and stir, scraping up any browned bits from the bottom of the pot, then let it bubble for 30 seconds or so. Add the crushed tomatoes, roasted red peppers, coriander, turmeric, 1 teaspoon salt, and ¼ teaspoon black pepper. Bring to a simmer, then reduce the heat to low and cook at a gentle simmer, stirring occasionally, until the mixture thickens to a chunky sauce, about 20 minutes. Season to taste with more salt and black pepper.

Add the roasted cauliflower to the tomato sauce and gently toss to coat. Top with as much of the tahini sauce and dukkah as you like, then sprinkle with the herbs and serve.

Brussels Sprouts Salad with Grapes, Pecorino, and Date-Pecan Dressing

Brussels sprouts look like baby cabbages, so why not treat them that way? When they're in season and especially sweet and tender, I thinly slice the raw veg and add ingredients that evoke cozy post-summer flavors, like juicy grapes and pecans, dried dates and maple syrup, with shavings of sheepy, salty pecorino to keep the sweetness in check. Come fall, some version of this salad is in our grab-and-go case at Playa and, thanks to those sturdy leaves, it doesn't sog out.

SERVES 4

For the dressing

⅓ cup raw pecans
¼ cup sherry vinegar
1 medium shallot, minced
¼ cup extra-virgin olive oil
2 tablespoons finely chopped pitted Medjool dates
1 tablespoon pure maple syrup
1 teaspoon whole-grain mustard
1 teaspoon kosher salt
¼ teaspoon freshly ground black pepper

For the salad

1 pound Brussels sprouts, bottoms trimmed and blemished leaves removed
2 cups sliced seedless red grapes
1 cup shaved Pecorino Romano cheese (I use a vegetable peeler)
Big handful of parsley (leaves and thin stems), chopped

Make the dressing

Preheat the oven to 350°F.

Spread the pecans over a baking sheet. Toast in the oven, shaking the pan once or twice, until fragrant and a shade or two darker, 8 to 10 minutes. Coarsely chop them and set aside.

Combine the vinegar and shallots in a small bowl and let the shallots hang out in the vinegar for a few minutes to soften their sharpness. Add the remaining dressing ingredients, including the chopped pecans, and whisk to combine.

Make the salad

Slice the Brussels sprouts into thin rings. Put them in a serving bowl and use your fingers to separate the rings into strips. Add the grapes, pecorino, and parsley and toss well.

Give the dressing another whisk, then add it to the salad and toss well. Season to taste with salt and pepper and serve.

Charred Red Cabbage with Fish Sauce, Orange, and Ginger

Red cabbage isn't just for slaw. When you cut it into wedges and give it some deep, open-the-kitchen-windows-level char, the pedestrian vegetable becomes remarkable: The interior tender, almost silky, and the edges crispy, the sweetness of cooked cabbage tempered by the slightly bitter char.

From there you can go in so many directions—yogurt sauce, salsa macha—though this preparation has become a fave. At Playa we often have an orange-laced version of nước chấm (the bright, umami-packed Vietnamese dipping sauce) on hand to serve with raw scallops. Here I pour it on those charred wedges before baking and it sneaks between the leaves to flavor the cabbage inside and out and turns sticky and saucy in the oven.

SERVES 4

For the nước chấm

¼ cup unseasoned rice vinegar
3 tablespoons fish sauce
Finely grated zest of 1 navel orange
Juice of 2 navel oranges
2 tablespoons sugar
2 garlic cloves, grated on a Microplane
1 teaspoon grated fresh ginger
1 Fresno chile or another moderately spicy fresh red chile, seeded and thinly sliced

For the cabbage

6 tablespoons neutral oil, like canola
1 large red cabbage, bruised outer leaves removed, cut into 6 wedges through the core
2 teaspoons kosher salt
¼ teaspoon freshly ground black pepper
Handful of cilantro (leaves and tender stems), chopped
2 scallions, thinly sliced

Make the nước chấm

Combine all the nước chấm ingredients in a medium bowl and stir to combine. Set aside.

Make the cabbage

Preheat the oven to 400°F.

Put a large cast-iron or other heavy-bottomed skillet over high heat until it starts to smoke. Add half the oil and give the pan a quick swirl to coat, then add half the cabbage wedges. Cook, flipping once, until the cut sides are deeply charred, 4 to 5 minutes. Transfer to a baking dish large enough to hold the wedges in a single layer (a little overlap is fine) and repeat with the remaining oil and cabbage.

Season the wedges on both sides with the salt and pepper, then pour the nước chấm over the cabbage, letting it pool in the bottom of the baking dish. Cover tightly with aluminum foil and bake, rotating the dish once halfway through, for 20 minutes. Remove the foil and bake until the sauce reduces to a syrup glaze and the cabbage is silky soft but still holds its shape, 15 minutes or so more.

Let the cabbage cool slightly in the baking dish, then spoon on some of the nước chấm. Garnish with the cilantro and scallions and serve.

STARCHY AND SWEET

Roots, Tubers, and Squash

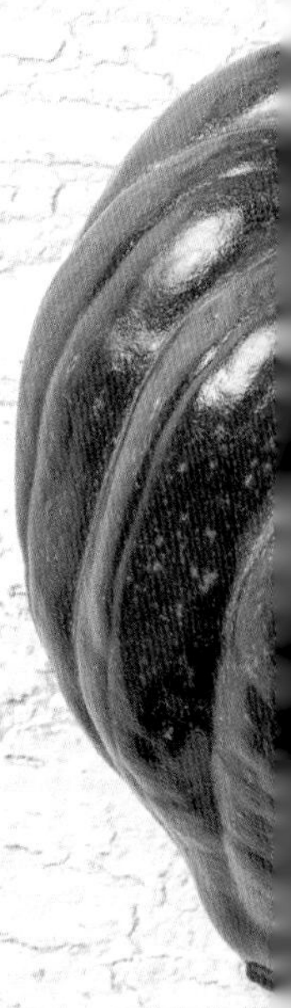

Maple-Miso Roasted Acorn Squash with Pumpkin Seed Dressing

This is a riff on a dish I've eaten my whole life: my mom's acorn squash roasted with butter and brown sugar. She was a health nut, so this felt extra special, like she was letting us eat dessert for dinner. In my kitchen, maple syrup and miso team up for complex sweetness with savory undertones. I also deploy a balsamic dressing, also from my mom's '90s repertoire, that provides just the right acidity to invigorate your palate and includes pumpkin seeds and nutty pumpkin seed oil to accentuate that earthy squash flavor.

SERVES 4

For the dressing

2 tablespoons balsamic vinegar
1 small shallot, minced
2 tablespoons pumpkin seed oil
1 tablespoon pure maple syrup
1 teaspoon whole-grain mustard
¼ cup pumpkin seeds, toasted and coarsely chopped
½ teaspoon kosher salt

For the squash

2 acorn squash (about 1¼ pounds each), halved through the stem and seeded
2 tablespoons extra-virgin olive oil
1 teaspoon kosher salt
¼ teaspoon freshly ground black pepper
3 tablespoons pure maple syrup
2 tablespoons shiro (white) miso paste
Big pinch of finely chopped fresh sage
3 tablespoons unsalted butter, cut into a dozen or so pieces
1 teaspoon flaky sea salt, like Maldon, for serving

For the fried sage

¼ cup neutral oil, like canola
12 large fresh sage leaves
½ teaspoon flaky sea salt, like Maldon

Make the dressing

Put the vinegar and shallot in a small bowl and let them hang out for a few minutes to soften the shallot's sharpness. Whisk in the pumpkin seed oil, maple syrup, mustard, pumpkin seeds, and salt and set aside.

Roast the squash

Preheat the oven to 375°F. Line a large baking dish with parchment paper.

Slice a little bit off the rounded side of the squash halves, just so they can sit upright without rocking. Put the squash in the prepared baking dish, cut-side up, brush or rub the flesh side with the olive oil, and season with the kosher salt and pepper.

Stir together the maple syrup, miso, and sage in a small bowl and pour the mixture into the squash cavities. Put the butter into the cavities, too, dividing it evenly. Roast, basting the squash with the butter mixture a few times as it cooks, until the flesh of the squash is soft and brown at the edges, 55 to 65 minutes.

Fry the sage

Ten minutes or so before the squash is done, heat the oil in a medium saucepan over medium heat until hot but not smoking. Add half the sage leaves and fry until crisp (they'll stop bubbling when they're done), 15 to 30 seconds. Use a slotted spoon to transfer the fried sage leaves to paper towels to drain. Immediately sprinkle with flaky salt and set aside. Repeat to fry the remaining sage.

Serve the dish

Remove the squash from the oven and let cool slightly, then halve each piece through the stem. Transfer to a serving platter, cut-side up, and spoon any buttery goodness left in the baking dish over the top. Give the dressing a quick whisk, then spoon it over the squash, garnish with the fried sage and some flaky salt, and serve.

Salt-and-Vinegar Duck Fat–Roasted Potatoes

These roasted potatoes can upstage even the most luscious leg of lamb or succulent piece of fish. Boiled in water with lots of salt (to season them throughout) and baking soda (which helps the exterior crisp up in the oven), the potatoes then get jostled in a bowl to fluff up their outsides. By the time you've roasted them in fragrant, glorious duck fat, the shaggy edges have become craggy, crunchy, and irresistible.

Stop there and you've got a winner, or take the potatoes to the next level, tossing them in a mixture of fennel pollen (for a delicate, floral fennel flavor) and vinegar powder (easy to find and an amazing addition to your pantry), which gives them total salt-and-vinegar-chip vibes. If you have leftover aioli (page 108), it makes a perfect dip.

SERVES 4

For the potatoes

Kosher salt
1 teaspoon baking soda
2½ pounds Yukon Gold potatoes, cut into 1-inch pieces
¼ cup rendered duck fat or extra-virgin olive oil
2 garlic cloves, smashed and peeled
3 thyme sprigs
1 rosemary sprig
4 large fresh sage leaves

For the spice mix

¼ teaspoon kosher salt
¼ teaspoon freshly ground black pepper
1 teaspoon vinegar powder
½ teaspoon fennel pollen or ¼ teaspoon ground fennel seeds
½ teaspoon garlic powder
½ teaspoon sugar

Make the potatoes

Preheat the oven to 425°F. Line a large baking sheet with parchment paper (or a silicone baking mat, if you have one).

Bring a large pot of water to a boil, salt it generously (like pasta water), and stir in the baking soda. Add the potatoes and cook, stirring occasionally, until you can easily slide a knife in and out of the potatoes, 8 to 10 minutes. Drain the potatoes well, put them in a single layer on a large baking sheet, and let them hang out until they stop steaming.

Combine the duck fat, garlic, and herbs in a medium skillet and let them sizzle over medium heat until the garlic has a touch of color, a minute or two, to infuse their flavor into the fat.

Put the potatoes back into the empty pot and toss until a film of potato starts to come off on the sides of the pot and the potatoes look shaggy. Add the rendered duck fat (with the garlic and herbs, too) and toss to coat well.

Spread the potatoes over the prepared baking sheet in a single layer and roast, tossing halfway through, until all the edges are golden and the potatoes are super crisp, 45 minutes to 1 hour.

Make the spice mix

While the potatoes are roasting, stir together all the spice mix ingredients in a small bowl.

As soon as the potatoes are done, sprinkle them with the spice mix, toss, and serve.

Crispy Sweet Potatoes with Red Curry Labneh and Sweet Fish Sauce Drizzle

Compared to white potatoes, giving sweet potatoes some texture requires a little extra effort. Here they're baked, then torn, and finally roasted so the pieces are enticingly crisp at the edges. A drizzle of sticky, funky sauce and dollops of tangy, spicy yogurt electrify each bite.

SERVES 4 TO 6

For the fish sauce drizzle

2 teaspoons extra-virgin olive oil
1 small shallot, minced
½ cup sugar
¼ cup plus 2 tablespoons fish sauce
½ teaspoon freshly ground black pepper

For the sweet potatoes

4 medium sweet potatoes (about 2 pounds), scrubbed
½ cup melted coconut oil or avocado oil
1 teaspoon flaky sea salt, like Maldon

For the labneh

½ cup labneh or plain full-fat Greek yogurt
2 teaspoons Thai red curry paste (Maesri brand is solid)
Finely grated zest and juice of 1 lime
½ teaspoon kosher salt
Handful of cilantro, chopped, for garnish

Make the fish sauce drizzle

Heat the olive oil in a medium saucepan over medium-low heat until it shimmers. Add the shallots and cook, stirring occasionally, until translucent, about 2 minutes. Add the sugar, fish sauce, and ½ cup water, then raise the heat to high and bring to a simmer, stirring to help the sugar dissolve.

Reduce the heat to medium and simmer until the mixture thickens and has the consistency of warm honey, 8 to 10 minutes. Stir in the black pepper, remove from the heat, and cool to room temperature.

The fish sauce drizzle keeps in the fridge for up to 3 weeks.

Roast the sweet potatoes

Preheat the oven to 400°F.

Poke holes all over the sweet potatoes with a fork and put them on a baking sheet. Bake until fully tender, 50 to 55 minutes. Remove from the oven and set aside until they're cool enough to handle. Keep the oven on.

Line two large baking sheets with parchment paper (or silicone baking mats, if you have them). Trim the ends off the sweet potatoes, then cut each one crosswise into 6 to 8 slices. Put them on the prepared baking sheets, leaving some space between the pieces. Use the bottom of a small bowl, jar, or small skillet to gently press down on each piece to flatten it a bit.

Brush the potatoes on both sides with the coconut oil and sprinkle with flaky salt. Roast, flipping once halfway through, until browned and crisp on both sides, 20 to 30 minutes.

Make the labneh and serve

Stir together the labneh, curry paste, lime zest, lime juice, and salt in a small bowl until smooth.

Arrange the sweet potatoes on a serving plate, drizzle with about ¼ cup of the fish sauce drizzle (or more to taste), and dollop with the labneh. Garnish with the cilantro and serve.

Bacon Fat–Roasted Parsnips with Brandy-Soaked Apricots and Pistachio Gremolata

I'm not a "bacon makes everything better" person. Its strong flavor tends to steal the spotlight. But because parsnips—which, by the way, are my nominee for top root vegetable—have so much character themselves, the smoky, porky fat enhances rather than overwhelms them, letting their distinctive sweetness shine. Providing a welcome foil are chewy booze-soaked apricots and pistachios mixed with herbs, lemon zest, and crisp bits of bacon.

SERVES 4

For the apricots

¼ cup brandy or cognac
3 tablespoons sugar
2 tablespoons apple cider vinegar
½ teaspoon kosher salt
¼ teaspoon ground or freshly grated nutmeg
2 star anise pods
½ cup sliced dried apricots

For the parsnips

1 tablespoon extra-virgin olive oil
4 or 5 slices bacon
2 pounds parsnips, peeled and cut into roughly 4 by ½-inch pieces
1 teaspoon kosher salt

For the gremolata

¼ cup chopped unsalted roasted pistachios
Handful of parsley, chopped
Finely grated zest of 1 lemon
1 tablespoon fried garlic, store-bought
1 tablespoon extra-virgin olive oil
Big pinch of flaky sea salt, like Maldon

(continued)

Make the apricots

Put the brandy, sugar, vinegar, salt, nutmeg, star anise, and 3 tablespoons water in a small saucepan over medium heat. Bring the mixture to a boil, add the apricots, then turn off the heat. Let the apricots soak for at least an hour.

Use a slotted spoon to transfer the apricots to a small bowl. Bring the liquid left in the pan to a simmer over medium heat and cook until it reduces to become slightly syrupy, like warm honey, 6 to 8 minutes. Remove from the heat, stir in the apricots, and cool to warm or room temp.

Roast the parsnips

Preheat the oven to 400°F. Line a large baking sheet with parchment paper (or a silicone baking mat, if you have one).

Put the olive oil in a skillet, add the bacon, and cook over medium-low heat, flipping once, until crispy, about 5 minutes. Transfer the bacon to paper towels to drain, reserving the fat in the pan. Finely chop the bacon and set aside for the gremolata.

Pour the rendered bacon fat into a large bowl, add the parsnips and salt, and toss with tongs to coat. Transfer the parsnips to the prepared baking sheet in an even layer, cover with aluminum foil, and roast for 15 minutes. Remove the foil, give the parsnips a toss, and roast until they're golden brown and tender, 20 to 25 minutes more.

Make the gremolata and serve

Stir together all the gremolata ingredients, along with the chopped bacon, in a medium bowl.

Lay the parsnips on a serving platter and top with about half the apricots and a drizzle of the syrup. Garnish with about half the gremolata (or more to taste) and serve.

Roasted Baby Beets with Burrata, Crispy Prosciutto, and Tangerine Dressing

I started cooking in the golden age of the beet and goat cheese salad, when (in California, at least) you rarely saw one without the other. And for good reason. Beets have a dense, earthy sweetness that goes so well with something creamy. Here I lean in but opt for cheese that's even more luxuriously creamy but milder in flavor, so the dish is more about the beets. Shards of crisped prosciutto and a dressing full of juicy citrus make this party a rager.

SERVES 4 TO 6

For the dressing

2 tablespoons red wine vinegar
2 tablespoons honey
1 teaspoon whole-grain mustard
1 teaspoon kosher salt
1 medium shallot, minced
3 tangerines or small sweet oranges
2 tablespoons extra-virgin olive oil

For the salad

30 or so baby beets, trimmed and scrubbed
3 tablespoons extra-virgin olive oil
1 teaspoon kosher salt
2 large rosemary sprigs
6 to 8 thin slices prosciutto
4 to 6 ounces burrata cheese
½ teaspoon flaky sea salt, like Maldon
¼ teaspoon freshly ground black pepper
Small handful of basil leaves (I love Greek basil here, but you do you), torn

Make the dressing

Combine the vinegar, honey, mustard, salt, and shallots in a medium bowl. Use a Microplane to finely grate the zest of the tangerines into the bowl. Whisk well, then slowly pour in the olive oil, whisking as you do.

Cut the ends off the tangerines to reveal the flesh, then carve off the peel and pith. Hold them over the bowl, then cut the segments from the membrane, letting them fall into the bowl. When you're done, squeeze in the juice from the membranes. Toss well and set aside.

(continued)

Make the salad and serve

Preheat the oven to 375°F. Position racks in the upper and lower thirds of the oven.

Put the beets in a large baking dish (one in which they fit in a crowded single layer), toss them with the olive oil, and season with the kosher salt. Nestle in the rosemary and pour in 2 tablespoons water. Cover with aluminum foil and bake on the lower rack, rotating the dish once halfway through, until you can insert a small sharp knife into the beets with no resistance, 45 to 55 minutes.

Meanwhile, line a large baking sheet with parchment paper (or a silicone baking mat, if you have one) and lay the prosciutto slices on top in a single layer. Bake on the upper rack, rotating the baking sheet once, until the prosciutto is cracker-crisp, 10 to 15 minutes. Let the prosciutto cool completely, then break each piece into a few shards.

When the beets are ready, remove the baking dish from the oven, take off the foil, and let the beets sit until they're cool enough to handle. Using a paper towel, rub the skins off the beets, halve or quarter them, and set aside in a large bowl.

Give the dressing another gentle toss or two and add half of it to the beets. Toss to coat, then season to taste with salt.

Break the burrata into a few pieces, put it on a serving plate, and sprinkle on the flaky salt and pepper. Top the burrata with the beets, then spoon the remaining dressing over the top. Garnish with the basil and the crispy prosciutto shards and serve.

BONUS COCKTAIL

Tangerine French 75

MAKES 2 DRINKS

1 ounce (2 tablespoons) honey
4 ounces (½ cup) strong brewed Earl Grey tea, hot
3 ounces (¼ cup plus 2 tablespoons) gin
2 ounces (¼ cup) fresh tangerine juice
4 ounces (½ cup) Champagne or other sparkling wine
2 tangerine twists, for garnish (optional, but swanky!)
Ice cubes

Put two 6- to 8-ounce coupe or martini glasses in the freezer to chill.

Stir the honey into the tea while it's hot. Set aside to cool completely.

Combine the gin, tangerine juice, and tea mixture in a container and stir well. For each drink, pour half the gin mixture into an ice-filled cocktail shaker and shake, then strain into one of the chilled glasses.

Top each glass with Champagne, garnish with the tangerine twists, if desired, and serve.

Honeynut Squash Risotto with Hazelnuts, Shallots, and Goat Brie

Honeynut squash isn't just adorable. Sure, it's less than half the size of its butternut cousin, but packs at least twice the flavor. That intense earthy, nutty sweetness is the focus of this risotto and comes in the form of both roasty cubes and a buttery puree you fold in to make the rice especially creamy. Silky bites of slow melting goat Brie boost the richness, and I garnish with shallots caramelized in hazelnut oil for a savory-sweet-nutty treat.

SERVES 4

For the squash

- 2 or 3 honeynut squash, or 1 small butternut squash (about 1¾ pounds total)
- 2 tablespoons extra-virgin olive oil
- 1 teaspoon kosher salt
- Freshly ground black pepper
- 3 tablespoons unsalted butter
- 1 tablespoon light brown sugar

For the shallots

- 2 tablespoons hazelnut oil or extra-virgin olive oil
- 1 cup thinly sliced shallots (2 to 3 large)
- ½ teaspoon kosher salt
- ¼ teaspoon granulated sugar

For the risotto

- ¼ cup hazelnuts
- 2 tablespoons unsalted butter
- 1 medium shallot, minced
- 1½ cups Arborio rice
- 4 thyme sprigs
- ½ cup dry white wine
- 2 teaspoons kosher salt
- 4 cups unsalted chicken stock or vegetable stock, warm
- 4 ounces goat Brie or regular Brie cheese, cubed

Cook the squash

Preheat the oven to 400°F.

Cut off the squash stems and halve the squash crosswise to separate the part with seeds from the part without. Peel the part without seeds and cut it into ½-inch cubes. Halve the other part lengthwise and scoop out the seeds and pulp. Put the unpeeled squash and the peeled cubes on opposite sides of a large baking sheet. Drizzle both with the oil, season with the salt and pepper to taste, and toss to coat.

Roast, stirring once halfway through, until the cubes are tender with a slight bite and a bit of color, 20 to 30 minutes. Transfer the cubes to a plate and set aside. If necessary, continue roasting the rest of the squash until very tender, 10 to 15 minutes more. Let the unpeeled squash cool slightly, then scoop the flesh into a food processor or blender, add the butter and sugar, and process until smooth. Set aside.

(continued)

Make the shallots

Heat a medium skillet over medium heat, add the hazelnut oil, and swirl to coat the surface of the pan. Add the shallots and salt and cook, stirring occasionally to start and more frequently as they brown, until very soft and sweet, 10 to 15 minutes.

Add the sugar and cook, stirring frequently and adding a splash of water if anything threatens to burn, until the shallots are a deep golden brown color, about 5 minutes more. Season to taste with more salt and set aside.

Make the risotto

Toast the hazelnuts in a small skillet over medium heat, stirring occasionally, until fragrant, 4 to 5 minutes. Coarsely chop and set aside.

Melt the butter in a large saucepan or medium Dutch oven over medium-low heat. Add the shallot and cook, stirring, until translucent, 2 to 3 minutes. Add the rice and thyme and cook, stirring frequently, until the rice is slightly golden and smells nutty, 2 to 3 minutes.

Increase the heat to medium, add the wine, and cook, stirring frequently, until it has evaporated, about 1 minute. Add the salt and just enough warm stock to cover the rice and cook, stirring frequently and occasionally scraping down the sides of the pan, until the stock has mostly been absorbed by the rice. Continue to add the stock a ladleful at a time, stirring and waiting until it's been absorbed before adding more, until you've added all the stock and the rice is tender with a nice bite, 20 to 25 minutes. Remove the thyme sprigs.

Reduce the heat to low and fold in the squash puree. Season to taste with salt and pepper, then fold in the cubed roasted squash. Serve in shallow bowls garnished with the hazelnuts, Brie, and caramelized shallots.

Root Vegetable Rösti with Poached Eggs and Grainy Mustard Hollandaise

One of my first jobs in a professional kitchen was at Fenix in LA working for chef Ken Frank, and at the time, he was known for his potato rösti. Swiss in origin, rösti is a spectacular puck of shredded potato (and nothing but shredded potato) with an incredible texture—crunchy on the outside and creamy and shreddy inside, like the hash brown of your dreams.

My patties tap into those pleasures while highlighting the many flavors of cold weather vegetables—the sweetness of carrot and parsnips, the radishy bite of turnips. Frank topped his rösti with caviar. I go for eggs of another sort, treating my root vegetable version as the bed for eggs Benedict with a light, bright hollandaise.

SERVES 4

For the rösti

1 cup coarsely grated carrot (about 1 large)
1 cup coarsely grated peeled parsnip (about 1 large)
1 cup coarsely grated peeled russet potato (about 1 large)
½ cup coarsely grated peeled turnip (about 1 medium)
⅓ cup coarsely grated yellow onion (about ½ medium)
2 teaspoons kosher salt, plus more for seasoning
¼ cup cornstarch
Neutral oil, like canola, for shallow-frying

For the hollandaise

2 sticks (1 cup) unsalted butter
4 large egg yolks
2½ teaspoons lemon juice, plus more to taste
1 teaspoon chopped fresh tarragon
2 teaspoons whole-grain mustard
1 teaspoon kosher salt, plus more as needed

For serving

4 large eggs, poached or cooked however you like

Make the rösti

Preheat the oven to 200°F. Line a baking sheet with paper towels.

Combine the grated vegetables and the onion in a colander, sprinkle on the salt, and toss well. Set the colander in the sink and let stand for 10 minutes to draw some of the liquid from the vegetables. Firmly squeeze the mixture a handful at a time to extract and drain as much liquid as possible, then add the mixture to a large bowl, discarding the liquid. Add the cornstarch and toss well.

Heat an inch or so of the oil in a large cast-iron or nonstick skillet over medium heat until it registers 350°F on a deep-fry or candy thermometer. Form the vegetable mixture into 4 patties that are about 1 inch thick, sliding them into the hot oil as you form them, and cook, flipping once, until golden brown and crispy on both sides, 8 to 10 minutes. Transfer the fried patties to the prepared baking sheet to drain and immediately season lightly with salt. Keep them warm in the oven while you make the hollandaise.

Make the hollandaise

Heat the butter in a small pot until completely melted and bubbling.

Combine the egg yolks, lemon juice, tarragon, and mustard in a blender. Blend the ingredients on low speed to start, gradually increasing the speed to high. Remove the stopper in the lid and, while the blender is running, carefully add in the hot butter in a thin, steady stream. Add the salt and blend briefly, gradually adding up to 2 tablespoons warm water if necessary to make a glossy, drizzle-able sauce. Season to taste with salt and lemon juice.

Top the rösti with the eggs, spoon on the hollandaise, and serve.

Carrot-Glazed Carrots with Coconut Milk and Seedy Za'atar Granola

Carrot lovers, this one's for you. Cooking carrots in their own juice cranks up the volume on their flavor. Molasses accentuates the sweetness even as its bitter edge tames it. As you may have noticed by now, I almost always crave crunch, so I shower the whole thing with a granola full of nuts, seeds, and the carrot-friendly herbs and spices in the Middle Eastern seasoning blend za'atar.

SERVES 4

1 pound trimmed small carrots, peeled or well scrubbed
1½ tablespoons coconut oil
1 medium shallot, minced
¾ cup carrot juice
2 teaspoons molasses or honey
1½ teaspoons kosher salt, plus more as needed
⅓ cup full-fat coconut milk
A good squeeze of lime juice
Freshly ground black pepper
½ cup Seedy Za'atar Granola (recipe follows)

Cut any especially fat carrots in half lengthwise. Otherwise, leave them whole.

Heat the coconut oil in a large skillet over medium-low heat for a minute or two. Add the carrots and shallot and cook, stirring occasionally, until the shallot is translucent, 3 to 4 minutes.

Add the carrot juice, molasses, and salt, increase the heat to medium, and shake the pan to coat the carrots in the liquid. Cook at a gentle simmer, shaking the pan occasionally, until the carrots are nearly tender and the carrot liquid thickens enough to look glazy, 8 to 10 minutes. If the carrots are tender before the liquid has thickened sufficiently, remove them from the pan and increase the heat for a bit.

Add the coconut milk to the pan and cook for 2 minutes more, shaking the pan to emulsify the sauce. Turn off the heat and stir in the lime juice. Season to taste with salt and pepper.

Transfer to a serving plate, sprinkle on the granola, and serve.

(continued)

Seedy Za'atar Granola

This granola recipe makes about four times what you'll need for the dish, but it's a great savory crunch to add to salads, or really anything that you want to add a nutty crunch to . . . so I say we make it a thing.

MAKES ABOUT 1½ CUPS

½ cup rolled oats
¼ cup raw walnuts, coarsely chopped
¼ cup raw hulled pumpkin seeds (pepitas)
¼ cup raw hulled sunflower seeds
2 tablespoons raw hemp hearts
2 tablespoons raw flaxseeds
1 tablespoon raw white sesame seeds
1 tablespoon raw black sesame seeds
2 tablespoons coconut oil, melted
1 tablespoon honey
1 teaspoon soy sauce
1½ teaspoons za'atar
¾ teaspoon kosher salt
¼ teaspoon freshly ground black pepper

Preheat the oven to 325°F. Line a large baking sheet with parchment paper.

Combine the oats, walnuts, pumpkin seeds, sunflower seeds, hemp hearts, flaxseeds, and sesame seeds in a large bowl and toss to combine.

Combine the melted coconut oil, honey, and soy sauce in a small bowl and stir well. Drizzle the honey mixture over the oat mixture and toss well. Sprinkle on half of the za'atar, toss to combine, then sprinkle on the remaining za'atar, the salt, and pepper and toss again.

Spread the mixture over the prepared baking sheet and bake, stirring once or twice, until toasty and a couple shades darker, about 20 minutes. Let cool before serving or storing.

The granola will keep in an airtight container in a cool, dry place for up to 5 days.

Carrot Farro with Chicken Skin Gremolata

I can't remember the first time I cooked farro in carrot juice. I think that's because I've done it so many times since. It's that good. As those nutty whole grains cook, the juice mingles with the starch in the farro to become creamy and concentrates to intensify that singular carroty-ness. To rein in the sweetness, there's Parm, chicken bouillon (bouillon was always in my parents' pantry for my dad's favorite predinner drink, the Bloody Bull), and an exhilarating topping headlined by crisped-up chicken skin.

SERVES 4 TO 6

- 1½ cups uncooked pearled farro
- 5 cups carrot juice
- 1 tablespoon light brown sugar
- 2 teaspoons kosher salt, plus more as needed
- 2 tablespoons extra-virgin olive oil
- 1 large leek, white and pale green parts only, halved lengthwise, cleaned, and thinly sliced
- 4 medium garlic cloves, thinly sliced
- ¾ teaspoon fennel seeds
- 2 chicken bouillon cubes
- ¼ teaspoon red chile flakes
- 1 large bunch spigarello, woody bottoms trimmed, coarsely chopped, or 3 cups thinly sliced Tuscan kale
- 3 tablespoons lemon juice, plus more to taste
- ½ cup finely grated Parmesan cheese, plus more as needed
- 2 tablespoons unsalted butter
- ¼ cup Chicken Skin–Sunflower Seed Gremolata (recipe follows), or more to taste

Combine the farro, 3 cups water, 3 cups of the carrot juice, the sugar, and 1 teaspoon of the salt in a large pot and bring to a boil over medium heat. Reduce the heat to maintain a moderate simmer and cook, uncovered, until the farro is tender but still has a slight bite and the liquid is mostly gone, 30 to 35 minutes. Let it cool while you proceed.

Heat the olive oil in a large skillet over medium heat until it shimmers. Add the leek, garlic, and fennel seeds and cook, stirring occasionally, until the leek has softened, 4 to 6 minutes. Add the farro, including any remaining cooking liquid, along with the remaining 2 cups carrot juice, the bouillon cubes, and chile flakes and increase the heat to medium-high. Cook at a rapid simmer, stirring occasionally, until the liquid reduces to coat the farro but is still plenty saucy, about 8 minutes. Fold in the spigarello just to wilt it slightly. Turn off the heat.

Fold in the lemon juice, Parmesan, butter, and remaining 1 teaspoon salt and season to taste with more salt and lemon juice. Spoon on the gremolata, garnish with more Parmesan, and serve.

Note: If you spot spigarello, buy it. The leafy vegetable tastes like a cross between broccoli leaf and Tuscan kale and shows up in markets around the time that carrots seem like an appropriate centerpiece to a meal. Thinly sliced kale, Tuscan or otherwise, makes a great sub.

(continued)

Chicken Skin–Sunflower Seed Gremolata

MAKES ABOUT ½ CUP

1 teaspoon extra-virgin olive oil
2 ounces chicken skin (from 1 chicken breast), coarsely chopped
½ teaspoon kosher salt
½ teaspoon garlic powder
2 tablespoons unsalted raw hulled sunflower seeds
2 medium garlic cloves, grated on a Microplane
Finely grated zest of 1 lemon
1 teaspoon flaky sea salt, like Maldon
Freshly ground black pepper
Handful of parsley, finely chopped

Heat the oil in a small skillet over medium-low heat for a minute or so. Add the chicken skin and cook slowly, flipping it occasionally, until golden brown and almost fully crispy, about 10 minutes. Sprinkle on the salt and garlic powder, toss well, then transfer the skin to paper towels to drain, reserving any fat in the pan.

Add the sunflower seeds to the pan and cook, stirring, until toasty brown, 3 to 5 minutes. Take the pan off the heat, add the chicken skin, and toss well. Let cool to just above room temperature, then stir in the garlic, lemon zest, flaky salt, pepper, and parsley. Stir well, then let it all hang out in the warm pan for a minute or so. Use immediately.

Note: You can use chicken skin you remove from a chicken breast or whole bird. I've also had luck asking a butcher if they have any in the back that they'd sell me.

SUGAR

Sun-Kissed Treats

Chocolate-Beet Cake with Chocolate-Miso Frosting

What might read as novelty dessert is actually just decadent layer cake that's all the better for its two not-so-secret ingredients. If you didn't tell your guests that the especially moist crumb and the quiet earthy sweetness, which plays so well with chocolate, is thanks to beets, or that the salty, complex note in the icing comes from miso, they'd never know.

MAKES 1 THREE-TIERED CAKE

For the cake

Nonstick cooking spray or butter, for greasing
1¼ cups canola oil
1 cup granulated sugar
1 cup packed light brown sugar
6 large eggs
1 tablespoon pure vanilla extract
1 cup sour cream
½ cup mayonnaise
2 cups all-purpose flour
1 cup unsweetened Dutch-processed cocoa powder
1 tablespoon baking soda
1 teaspoon kosher salt
¾ cup beet juice
¾ cup buttermilk

For the frosting

3 sticks (1½ cups) unsalted butter, at room temp
1 tablespoon shiro (white) miso paste
4½ cups confectioners' sugar
¾ cup unsweetened Dutch-processed cocoa powder
¼ cup full-fat coconut milk

Make the cake

Preheat the oven to 350°F. Spray the bottom and sides of three 8-inch round cake pans or grease with butter, then line the bottoms with circles of parchment paper cut to fit.

In the bowl of a stand mixer fitted with the paddle attachment, combine the oil, granulated sugar, and brown sugar and beat on medium speed until smooth, lighter in color, and fluffy, 2 to 3 minutes. With the mixer running, add the eggs one at a time, then the vanilla, and mix until combined. Add the sour cream and mayonnaise and mix until combined.

Sift the flour, cocoa powder, and baking soda into a medium bowl and whisk to combine. With the mixer on its lowest speed, add the dry ingredients in a few batches, waiting until each batch is incorporated before adding the next. Slowly pour in the beet juice and buttermilk and mix until smooth, scraping the bottom and sides with a flexible spatula to make sure there's no loose flour.

(continued)

Divide the batter evenly among the three prepared pans and bake, rotating their positions halfway through to make sure they cook evenly, until a toothpick inserted into the center of the cakes comes out clean, 25 to 30 minutes. Let them cool in the pans to room temp, at least 1 hour.

Make the frosting

While the cakes cool, clean and dry the stand mixer bowl and paddle attachment, then return them to the mixer. Combine the butter and miso in the mixer bowl and beat on low speed, gradually increasing the speed to medium-high, until the butter is light in color and fluffy in texture, 2 to 3 minutes.

Sift the confectioners' sugar and cocoa powder into a medium bowl and whisk to combine. With the mixer on its lowest speed, add the dry ingredients in a few batches, waiting until each batch is incorporated before adding the next. Slowly pour in the coconut milk, then gradually increase the speed to high and mix until the frosting is smooth, fluffy, and easily spreadable, about 1 minute.

Frost and serve.

Run a butter knife around the edges of the pans to release the cakes, then invert the cakes onto plates or a wire rack. Remove the parchment paper. Use a serrated knife to trim off the domed tops so that the cakes are flat (the scraps are great for snacking!).

Put the first layer of cake on a cake stand or large serving plate. Scoop about 1 cup of the frosting onto the cake and spread it evenly over the top (an offset spatula makes this easy). Put the second layer of cake on top of the first and frost it the same way. Finally, put the third layer of cake on top, bottom-side up, and frost the entire cake (sides first, then the top) with the remaining frosting. It's fun to try to make it as pretty as possible, but it doesn't have to look perfect to taste great.

Slice and serve. Store any leftovers, covered, in the fridge so they don't dry out, up to 3 days.

Vanilla-Chamomile Flan with Whatever Fruit Looks Great

Imagine this: You're competing in the finale of *Top Chef*, and your mom is there. You decide to make flan—the silky custard topped with a layer of caramel, to which you add a touch of chamomile for a floral back note. You made this for your dessert course because flan is your all-time favorite and in homage to your mom, who makes some of the best flan on the planet. Then, on camera, she takes one bite and announces that it could be better.

Now imagine if she were right. I did manage to win that season, but not because of my too-dense flan, the victim of an oven-temperature snafu. Hudson still gives me shit for it, so during the dark spring of 2020, when I had some unexpected time at home, I committed to proving that my flan game was on point. I made at least one flan a week for months and delivered them to friends. So, Mom, Hudson, this one's for you.

MAKES ONE 9-INCH FLAN

½ cup plus ⅔ cup sugar
3 large eggs, at room temp
3 large egg yolks, at room temp
1 teaspoon vanilla bean paste or pure vanilla extract
2 cups whole milk
1 cup heavy cream
2 chamomile tea bags
Fresh fruit (like sliced figs, persimmons, stone fruit, or berries), for serving

Combine ½ cup of the sugar and a scant ¼ cup water in a small saucepan, whisk well, and set over medium-low heat. Cook, without stirring, until the sugar dissolves and the mixture starts to bubble, then finally turns an amber color, 10 to 15 minutes.

Take it off the heat, give the caramel a quick swirl, and pour it over the bottom of a 9-inch round nonstick or ceramic baking pan, tilting the pan so it evenly coats the bottom. Let it cool to room temperature.

Make the flan

Preheat the oven to 350°F.

Whisk together the eggs, egg yolks, vanilla, and remaining ⅔ cup sugar in a large bowl until fully combined. Set aside.

Combine the milk, cream, and tea bags in a medium saucepan over medium-low heat. Bring the mixture to a gentle simmer, then remove the pan from the heat. Scoop out the tea bags, pressing them against the side of the pan with the back of a spoon to squeeze as much liquid from them as you can. Discard the tea bags.

(continued)

While whisking constantly, slowly pour about ¼ cup of the hot milk mixture into the egg mixture (adding the hot milk slowly at first helps ensure that you don't scramble the eggs). Add the rest of the milk in a steady stream, whisking as you do. Set aside.

Carefully pour the flan base into the pan on top of the cooled caramel. Gently pick up the pan and tap it a few times on the counter to pop any air bubbles inside the flan mixture. Set the pan inside a roasting pan or a very wide ovenproof pot. Carefully pour warm water into the larger pan until it reaches somewhere between halfway and two-thirds up the sides of the flan pan. Bake, uncovered, until the flan is set but still jiggly in the center, about 40 minutes.

Carefully remove the flan from the water bath and let it cool to room temperature. Cover and refrigerate until completely chilled, at least 6 hours or up to 2 days.

To unmold the flan, run a paring knife around the edge of the pan to loosen it a bit, then invert a larger plate or platter on top of the flan. In one fluid (and confident!) maneuver, flip both the plate and the pan so the flan releases onto the plate. If the flan doesn't immediately release, tap on the center of the pan until it does.

Top with the fresh fruit and serve.

Passion Fruit Curd Pie with Coconut-Sesame Crust and Honey Meringue

I know it's a living-in-LA flex, but there are almost too many passion fruits in my yard. Every summer, I harvest dozens and then get to work scooping and straining their pulp into bags destined for my freezer. That way, all year I can channel their bracingly tart, tropical-fruity flavor into rich, creamy curd. Don't you worry if you lack the vine—frozen, unsweetened puree is totally great, too.

Treat it like you would any fruit curd, topping it with fruit, slathering it on scones or biscuits (page 145), or if you're my son, eating it by the bowlful as if it were yogurt (which, Hudson, it very much is not). Or, of course, turning it into pie, preferably with this crust jazzed up with coconut and sesame. Get fancy with torched honey meringue on top or go for whipped cream sweetened with a touch of honey.

MAKES ONE 9-INCH PIE

For the passion fruit curd

- 2 teaspoons unflavored powdered gelatin (from a ¼-ounce envelope)
- 1⅓ cups frozen unsweetened passion fruit puree, thawed
- 1¼ cups granulated sugar
- 8 large eggs
- ¼ teaspoon pure vanilla extract
- 2 sticks (1 cup) unsalted butter, cut into 1-inch cubes, at room temp
- ¼ teaspoon kosher salt

For the coconut-sesame crust

- 2½ cups all-purpose flour, plus more for dusting
- 2 tablespoons unsweetened coconut flakes, lightly toasted
- 2 tablespoons toasted sesame seeds
- 1 tablespoon granulated sugar
- 1 teaspoon kosher salt
- 2 sticks (1 cup) cold unsalted butter, cut into 1-inch cubes
- ¼ cup ice water, plus more as needed
- Pie weights or dried beans

For the meringue

- 4 egg whites, at room temperature
- 1 teaspoon lemon juice
- ½ cup granulated sugar
- ½ cup honey

(continued)

Make the passion fruit curd

Combine the gelatin and 2 tablespoons water in a small bowl and let it sit for 5 minutes, so the gelatin powder has a chance to absorb the water.

Pour 2 inches or so of water into a medium pot and bring it to a simmer, then reduce the heat to maintain a gentle simmer. In a heatproof bowl large enough to sit over the pot without touching the water, combine the passion fruit puree, sugar, eggs, and vanilla. Set the bowl over the pot and cook, whisking almost constantly, until the mixture thickens to a custardy texture (usually soon after the froth subsides), 8 to 10 minutes. Add the gelatin mixture, butter, and salt and whisk vigorously (or blend with an immersion blender) until the butter has melted and the mixture is smooth.

Remove the bowl from the pot. Cover with plastic wrap, pressing it directly against the surface of the curd to prevent a skin from forming, and refrigerate for at least 4 hours to set or up to 3 days. Before using, give it a good whisk.

Make the coconut-sesame crust

Combine the flour, coconut flakes, sesame seeds, sugar, and salt in a food processor and pulse three or four times to mix. Add the butter and pulse until the mixture is crumbly, with pieces of butter a bit smaller than peas (the size of, say, lentils), about 15 times. Sprinkle ¼ cup of the ice water over the surface of the mixture and pulse a few more times, scraping the sides of the bowl between pulses to help distribute everything evenly. Check if the dough is ready by pinching some with your fingers: If it holds together, it's done. If it doesn't, add more ice water 1 tablespoon at a time, and pulse until the dough just comes together. Transfer the dough to a large sheet of plastic wrap. Press the dough with your palms to bring it together and form a rough rectangle. Wrap in the plastic wrap, and refrigerate for at least 1 hour or up to a day.

Assemble the pie

On a lightly floured surface, roll the dough into a ¼-inch-thick, roughly round shape. Lay the dough in a 9-inch pie dish and lightly press against the bottom and sides. Trim all but about ½ inch of the overhang and crimp the edges. Pop the pie crust in the freezer for 15 minutes to prevent shrinking in the oven.

Meanwhile, preheat the oven to 350°F. Line the pie crust with parchment paper and add pie weights or dried beans. Bake, rotating the dish once, until the edges of the crust are golden brown, about 15 minutes. Remove the parchment and weights. Prick the crust at the bottom all over with a fork. Bake again, rotating once, until the crust at the bottom is golden brown, about 15 minutes more. Let cool completely.

Whisk the passion fruit curd to loosen it, then spoon it into the crust and spread it into an even layer. Pop it in the fridge for 30 minutes.

Make the meringue

Combine the egg whites and lemon juice in the bowl of a stand mixer fitted with the whisk attachment. Whip on medium speed until soft peaks form, about 4 minutes. Meanwhile, whisk together the sugar, honey, and ½ cup water in a small saucepan and bring to a simmer over medium-high heat.

When the egg whites form soft peaks, reduce the mixer speed to low and slowly drizzle the hot sugar mixture into the egg whites (avoid pouring it onto the whisk attachment) until fully incorporated. Gradually increase the speed and whip until the egg whites hold stiff peaks. Let cool to room temperature.

Dollop the meringue over the top of the pie to completely cover the surface. If you've got a blowtorch, lightly torch the peaks until they're browned and toasty, then serve.

BONUS COCKTAIL

Spicy Passion Fruit–Cucumber Margarita

MAKES 4 DRINKS

About 2 tablespoons flaky sea salt, like Maldon
1 lime wedge
3 ripe passion fruits
1 Persian cucumber
1 fresh green chile, like a serrano, halved crosswise
1½ ounces (3 tablespoons) agave syrup
4 ounces (½ cup) mezcal
4 ounces (½ cup) blanco tequila
2 ounces (¼ cup) fresh lime juice
Ice cubes

Crumble the flaky salt onto a small plate. Use the lime wedge to moisten the rims of four 6- to 8-ounce rocks glasses. One by one, invert the glasses into the salt and turn to coat the rim. (I like to coat just half the rim, but coat the whole thing if you're feeling salty.) Turn them right-side up and set aside.

Halve each passion fruit and scoop the pulp and seeds into a blender. Cut several thin slices from the cucumber and set aside for garnish, then chop the rest and add it to the blender. Add half the chile and the agave and puree until pretty smooth. Strain the mixture into a container, then add the mezcal, tequila, and lime juice and stir well.

Fill the salt-rimmed glasses with ice. Thinly slice the remaining chile. For each drink, pour about a quarter of the passion fruit mixture into an ice-filled cocktail shaker and shake, then strain into one of the glasses. Garnish with the reserved cucumber and chile slices. Drink up.

Sticky Date Cake with Bourbon Toffee and Whipped Crème Fraîche

Just like dried dates themselves, this cake is moist, sticky, and on the verge of too sweet, which to me is actually one of its great pleasures. I yank it back from the brink with the tang of fluffy whipped crème fraîche and a little orange zest and bourbon (reminiscent of an old-fashioned) in the toffee sauce.

SERVES 4

For the sauce

¾ cup packed light brown sugar
½ cup heavy cream
¼ cup bourbon
⅛ teaspoon kosher salt
1 stick (½ cup) unsalted butter, cut into cubes
2 teaspoons vanilla bean paste or pure vanilla extract
Finely grated zest of 1 orange

For the date cake

Nonstick cooking spray or butter, for greasing
8 dried Medjool dates, pitted
¾ cup all-purpose flour
1 teaspoon baking powder
1 teaspoon kosher salt
¼ teaspoon baking soda
½ stick (4 tablespoons) unsalted butter, at room temp
¾ cup packed brown sugar
1 large egg
1 teaspoon vanilla bean paste or pure vanilla extract

For the crème fraîche

1 cup crème fraîche
3 tablespoons confectioners' sugar
½ teaspoon vanilla bean paste or pure vanilla extract

Make the sauce

Combine the sugar, cream, bourbon, and salt in a small saucepan, set it over low heat, and cook at a gentle simmer, stirring occasionally, until the sugar has dissolved and the sauce has thickened slightly, 10 to 12 minutes. Remove from the heat, then whisk in the butter, vanilla, and orange zest. Pour through a fine-mesh strainer into a heatproof container and keep warm.

(continued)

Make the cakes

Preheat the oven to 350°F with a rack in the center position. Grease four 6-ounce ramekins with the cooking spray or butter. Set them on a large baking sheet.

Put the dates in a small saucepan with ¾ cup water and simmer until most of the water has been absorbed and the dates are very soft, about 15 minutes. Transfer the dates and any liquid remaining in the pan to a blender or small food processor and puree until smooth, stopping to stir and scrape down the sides if necessary. Set aside.

Combine the flour, baking powder, salt, and baking soda in a small bowl.

Combine the butter and brown sugar in the bowl of a stand mixer fitted with the paddle attachment and beat on medium speed until lighter in color and fluffy. Add the egg, vanilla, and date puree and beat until fully combined. Reduce the speed to low, add the flour mixture and mix until fully combined.

Spoon the batter into the prepared ramekins and bake on the center rack, rotating the baking sheet once, until a toothpick inserted into the center of the cakes comes out mostly clean, about 20 minutes. Let the cakes cool for a few minutes.

Make the crème fraîche

Combine the crème fraîche, confectioners' sugar, and vanilla in the bowl of a stand mixer fitted with the whisk attachment (or just use a large bowl and a handheld mixer). Whip on low speed for a minute or so, then whip on high until the crème fraîche holds soft peaks, 1 to 2 minutes more.

Slide the cakes out of the ramekins and onto plates, smother in the toffee sauce, dollop with the crème fraîche, and serve.

Note: For an extra-sticky (in the best way) cake, try this: After removing the cakes from the ramekins, pour a few spoonfuls of the toffee sauce into each ramekin, return the cakes to the ramekins, and bake for another few minutes so the toffee sauce gets hot and infuses into the cakes. Remove the cakes from the ramekins again (you might need to use a knife to slide them out this time) and serve toffee-side up with more sauce and the crème fraîche.

Marinated Strawberries and Rhubarb with Whipped Yogurt and Pretzel-Pistachio Granola

Strawberry-rhubarb is my top pick for pie. That strawberry sweetness coupled with the rhubarb's specific tannic tartness makes for a filling that feels alive and exciting rather than sweet and flat. Marinated but not cooked to pay respect to high-season berries, this strawberry-rhubarb combo is so compelling, especially amped up with vanilla and black pepper, that you can ditch the crust. I do here in favor of granola with pistachio and pretzels to offset the sweetness and juicy texture. A yogurt topping is great, but whipped yogurt is better.

SERVES 4

For the strawberries and rhubarb

1 cup granulated sugar
1 vanilla bean, split lengthwise, then halved crosswise
1 teaspoon black peppercorns, coarsely ground
2 cups sliced rhubarb (sliced on an angle into ½-inch-thick pieces)
2 cups halved strawberries

For the granola

½ cup raw shelled pistachios, chopped
¼ cup raw hulled pumpkin seeds (pepitas)
¼ cup rolled oats
2 tablespoons raw sunflower seeds
1½ teaspoons raw black sesame seeds
1½ teaspoons raw flaxseeds
2 tablespoons unsalted butter, melted
1 tablespoon honey
¼ teaspoon kosher salt
½ cup coarsely chopped salted pretzels

For the whipped yogurt

1 cup plain full-fat Greek yogurt
½ cup heavy cream
3 tablespoons honey
¼ teaspoon kosher salt

(continued)

Marinate the strawberries and rhubarb

Combine the sugar and 1 cup water in a medium saucepan and bring to a simmer over medium-high heat, whisking until the sugar has fully dissolved. Remove the pan from the heat. Use the back of a paring knife to scrape out the seeds from one vanilla bean half (reserving the other half), then add the seeds and the scraped pod to the pan along with the pepper. Whisk well, then stir in the rhubarb and let steep until the liquid is completely cool.

Remove and discard the vanilla bean pod. Gently stir in the strawberries and let it all marinate at room temp for at least 1 hour or, preferably, in the fridge for 4 to 8 hours.

Make the granola

Preheat the oven to 300°F. Line a large baking sheet with parchment paper (or a silicone baking mat, if you have one).

Combine the pistachios, pumpkin seeds, oats, sunflower seeds, sesame seeds, and flaxseeds in a large bowl and toss well.

Combine the melted butter, honey, and salt in a small bowl, then scrape the seeds from the remaining vanilla bean half into the bowl and stir well. Drizzle the butter mixture over the pistachio mixture and toss to coat.

Spread the mixture over the prepared baking sheet in a single layer and bake, stirring occasionally so that everything cooks evenly, until toasty and a few shades darker, 25 to 35 minutes. Remove the pan from the oven, stir in the pretzels, and let cool completely.

Make the whipped yogurt

Put the yogurt, cream, honey, and salt in the bowl of a stand mixer fitted with the whisk attachment (or just use a large bowl and a handheld mixer). Whip on low speed for a minute or so, then whip on high until the mixture holds soft peaks, 1 to 2 minutes more.

Spoon the fruit and a little of the syrup into bowls, top with the yogurt and then the granola, and serve.

Sweet Corn Panna Cotta with Blackberries and Caramel Corn

Corn makes some of the most interesting and dynamic desserts. It can taste candy-sweet, but since it's typically served in a savory context (outside of some countries in Asia and Latin America, at least), its presence in this wonderfully wobbly, low-effort dessert is mind-bending, in a lovely way. Blackberries are a classic partner for corn, fragrant makrut lime leaf is not, but together they make magic, like the threesome you always wanted to watch. Yeah, you heard me.

SERVES 4

For the panna cotta

2 ears corn, preferably white, shucked
1½ cups whole milk
1 cup heavy cream
½ cup granulated sugar
¼ cup honey
1 teaspoon vanilla bean paste or pure vanilla extract
¼ teaspoon kosher salt
4 fresh makrut lime leaves, torn
1 (¼-ounce) envelope unflavored powdered gelatin (2¼ teaspoons)

For the topping

1 pint blackberries, halved lengthwise
2 tablespoons granulated sugar
¼ teaspoon finely grated lemon zest
1 tablespoon lemon juice
¼ teaspoon kosher salt
3 fresh makrut lime leaves, center ribs removed, very thinly sliced
About 1 cup caramel corn, for garnish

Make the panna cotta

Slice the corn kernels off the cobs, reserving the cobs. Transfer the kernels to a blender and puree until smooth, 1 to 2 minutes, gradually adding some of the milk to help it blend. Set a fine-mesh strainer over a medium saucepan and pour in the corn puree, pressing down on the corn with a spoon or rubber spatula to extract as much liquid as possible. Discard the solids. You should have about ½ cup of corn liquid.

Add the milk, cream, sugar, honey, vanilla, salt, and lime leaves and whisk well. Break the reserved corncobs in half and add them to the pan. Slowly bring the mixture to a simmer over low heat, then simmer very gently for 5 minutes. Remove the pan from the heat, cover, and let it steep for 10 minutes. Discard the cobs and keep warm.

Put 3 tablespoons water in a small bowl, sprinkle in the gelatin, and let it sit for 5 minutes so the gelatin powder has a chance to absorb the water. Whisk the gelatin mixture into the warm corn mixture until it's completely dissolved, then strain the mixture into a large container (something with a spout makes for easy pouring).

Line a baking sheet with a kitchen towel. Set four 8-ounce glass serving vessels (coupes or soufflé dishes work great) on the baking sheet. Fill each halfway with the corn mixture and refrigerate, uncovered, until set, about 4 hours. (Or, if not serving the panna cotta immediately, cover and refrigerate for up to 2 days.)

Make the topping and serve

Toss together the blackberries, sugar, lemon zest, lemon juice, salt, and lime leaves in a medium bowl. Let the mixture sit until the berries soften and release some juice, at least 20 minutes or up to 1 hour before serving.

Top the panna cotta with the blackberry mixture and caramel corn and serve immediately.

Stone Fruit–Amaretto Clafoutis with Cherry Compote

Is there an easier dessert in existence that tastes this luxurious? A countryside French treat, clafoutis starts as an easy, eggy batter that's poured over fruit. Once baked, however, it becomes so light and custardy that your guests will assume it took you all day to make.

Tweaked with just a touch of amaretto and orange zest, mine otherwise hews pretty close to the classic. Virtually any juicy fruit works, from berries to cherries, though stone fruit plays particularly nicely with the almondlike quality of the booze. Because clafoutis is so simple, I often get restless and whip up a totally optional, totally delicious cherry compote to serve alongside.

SERVES 6 TO 8

For the cherry compote

1 pound sweet cherries, pitted
¼ cup granulated sugar
1 teaspoon pure vanilla extract or vanilla bean paste
¼ cup lemon juice
2 teaspoons cornstarch
¼ teaspoon kosher salt

For the clafoutis

1 tablespoon unsalted butter, at room temp
2 large eggs
1 large egg yolk
1 cup whole milk
1 cup all-purpose flour
½ cup heavy cream
½ cup granulated sugar
1 tablespoon amaretto liqueur
½ teaspoon kosher salt
1 tablespoon finely grated orange zest
3 cups mixed sliced stone fruit (1-inch wedges)
Confectioners' sugar, for dusting

Make the compote

Combine the cherries, sugar, and vanilla in a medium saucepan, set over medium heat, and cook at a gentle simmer, stirring occasionally, until the cherries have released their juices and softened, 10 to 12 minutes.

Whisk together the lemon juice and cornstarch in a small bowl, add the mixture to the cherries, and cook, stirring constantly, until the liquid thickens enough to coat the back of a spoon, a minute or two. Remove the pan from the heat, stir in the salt, and let the compote cool to warm or room temperature. (Or let cool completely, transfer to an airtight container, and store in the fridge for up to 1 week. It's also great on French toast, pancakes, and ice cream.)

Make the clafoutis

Preheat the oven to 350°F with a rack in the center position. Grease the bottom and sides of a 9-inch round or square baking dish with the butter and set the baking dish on a large baking sheet.

Combine the eggs, egg yolk, milk, flour, cream, granulated sugar, amaretto, and salt in a blender. Blend, starting on low speed and gradually increasing the speed to high, until the batter is fully combined and slightly frothy, about 30 seconds. Add the orange zest and blend for another few seconds. Set aside.

Put the fruit in the prepared baking dish and spread it into an even layer, then pour in the batter. Bake on the center rack, rotating the baking sheet once halfway through, until the outer edges of the clafoutis are puffed and golden brown and the center no longer jiggles, 30 to 40 minutes.

Remove the clafoutis from the oven, dust it with confectioners' sugar, and serve right away, with the compote on the side for spooning over each portion.

My Favorite Chocolate Chip Cookies

There's nothing sun-kissed about these. They're just my absolute favorite cookies—crisp at the edges and soft in the middle, with big gooey chocolate chunks and flakes of sea salt on top. We served them at Playa from the beginning and still do to this day. We even sell the frozen dough in our grab-and-go case. Baking the cookies from frozen is actually the way to go to ensure the center is slightly, perfectly underdone. Plus, it means they're always on hand, whether you want to bake off two or two dozen.

MAKES 24 TO 26 LARGE COOKIES

3 sticks (1½ cups) unsalted butter, at room temp
1½ cups granulated sugar
1½ cups packed light brown sugar
3 large eggs
1 tablespoon pure vanilla extract
3½ cups all-purpose flour
1½ teaspoons baking soda
¾ teaspoon kosher salt
2½ cups semisweet chocolate chips, chunks, or discs
Flaky sea salt, like Maldon

Combine the butter and both sugars in the bowl of a stand mixer fitted with a paddle attachment and beat on medium speed, scraping down the sides halfway through, until smooth and fluffy, about 2 minutes. Reduce the mixer speed to low and add the eggs one at a time, waiting until each one is fully incorporated before adding the next. Add the vanilla and mix just until combined.

In a large bowl, combine the flour, baking soda, and salt and mix well. With the mixer on low speed, add the flour mixture about 1 cup at a time, mixing until each addition is incorporated and scraping down the sides of the bowl before adding the next. Raise the mixer speed to medium-high and beat until smooth with no lumps, 10 seconds or so. Fold in the chocolate chips by hand so they're evenly distributed.

Line a baking sheet with parchment paper (or a silicone baking mat, if you have one). Scoop heaping ¼-cup mounds of dough onto the prepared baking sheet, leaving a little space between each one. Freeze overnight, then transfer to resealable bags. Store in the freezer for up to 3 months.

Preheat the oven to 375°F with a rack in the center position. Line a large baking sheet with parchment paper.

Arrange 6 cookie dough balls on the prepared baking sheets, leaving at least 3 inches of space between them. Sprinkle a pinch of flaky salt over the top of each one. Bake on the center rack, rotating the pan halfway through, until the cookies are golden brown at the edges and just slightly underdone in the center, 15 to 17 minutes.

Bake more cookies, if you'd like, and serve them warm.

ACKNOWLEDGMENTS

Thank you to Hudson, my son and the incredible human responsible for the best job title I will ever hold. Thank you for being my taster and for your always-honest feedback. For motivating me to lead by example, for removing failure as an option, for understanding the roller coaster of my travel schedule (and moods), and my need for a hug the moment I return.

Thank you to Nick, though no paragraph could ever do justice to your contributions to my life, my career, or this book. Without you, none of what I love about my life would exist. For the past twenty-three years, you've held my hand through every terrifying, glorious step of our lives. You've sacrificed so much for my career. You gave me the courage and imagination to succeed. Oh, and you also laboriously and meticulously tested every recipe in this book. Our story together may have changed course, but you are and always will be my family and my best friend. My love and appreciation for you runs deeper than you will ever know.

To Mom and Dad, for a lifetime of fabulous food memories, for never limiting the possibilities, for supporting my every dream, and for your unconditional love. You two are the perfect example of how to love and live.

To Jessica, my protector since birth. Thank you for my first perfectly scrambled cream cheese eggs, for the security of true sisterhood, and for being the "good" daughter, so that I didn't have to be.

To Zach Field, the best manager in the biz (whatever this "biz" is anymore) and, more important, my friend. Thank you for the endless hours of professional and personal therapy, for organizing my entire world, for advocating tirelessly for me, for having all the right words in all the right moments. You're a wise man, Mr. Grumpy Pants. I'm so lucky to have you in my corner.

To Andrea Blatt, literary agent extraordinaire. Thank you for holding my hand through every email, pitch, meeting, and Zoom. For never losing faith and making sure the third time was the charm.

To JJ Goode, my coauthor, magician, mind reader, and friend. First, what would I do without you? Second, how does anyone write a book without you? Thank you for always knowing exactly what I mean, even when I can't articulate it. For keeping me on track, for understanding how overwhelmed I can get, and for feeding me next steps in baby bites so that I can properly digest. You're the reason I'm not absolutely thrilled that the arduous process of writing a cookbook is over, and the only reason I'd consider doing it again. Please don't ever leave me.

To Huge Galdones, a photographer with an eye like no other. Thank you for seeing the big picture (pun intended) and for bringing these recipes to life on the page. Your ability to capture the perfect moment is remarkable, and I couldn't be more thrilled with what we did together. And to Eric Lundy and Huxley McCorkle for your styling magic.

To Karen Rinaldi, Kirby Sandmeyer, Bonni Leon-Berman, Jessica Gilo, Olivia McGiff, Robin Billardello, and my entire team at Harper. I'm so lucky that I got to do this with a group of ladies who totally get it. You've not only made my book dream a reality, but you've transformed my half-formed thoughts and barely articulated vision into something so beautiful, a work of art I'll be proud of forever.

To the staff at Playa Provisions, a phenomenal bunch of misfits that I'm proud to call my family. TV chefs get all the credit, but you guys are the ones who make all the things happen. Thank you for caring as much as you do, every damn day.

To Bobby, my mentor and my friend. I'm constantly inspired by your ability to cook, create, and command, by how you work your ass off and enjoy life in equal measure. Thank you for always having my back, even when I'm too busy drowning in self-doubt to see straight. For pushing me to keep at it, even when I'm ready to give up. For your unabashedly honest, never-sugarcoated feedback, and, *totally* unrelated, for coming up with a better title for this damn book.

To my countless culinary mentors, the colleagues, cooks, sous chefs, and bosses I've learned so much from over the years. Special thanks to Ken Frank, for opening that first door for a nineteen-year-old with approximately zero experience, and to Michael McCarty for opening a million more.

To my *Top Chef* and Food Network families, to the people behind the scenes who make me look like I know what I'm doing on-screen. And to my culinary comrades and fellow competitors, who keep me sane and inspire (and terrify) me with their skill, so I stay sharp.

To my chosen family, the friends who I can laugh with and cry to, who never judge me or let me fall. You know who you are. That I can spend this life with you makes me the luckiest gal in the world.

And finally, to my Brooks running shoes, for the many miles of mind-clearing runs that kept me (half) sane during the past four or five years, some of the hardest and most rewarding of my life.

INDEX

ABOUT THE AUTHOR

Born and raised in Los Angeles, Brooke Williamson owns and operates the restaurant Playa Provisions with Nick Roberts. Brooke won Bravo's *Top Chef* Season 14 and the Food Network's *Tournament of Champions* Season 1. She is one of the three titans on the hit competition show *Bobby's Triple Threat*. Brooke loves running, playing tennis, and hanging in and out of the kitchen with her teenage son, Hudson.

FIRST EDITION

Designed by Bonni Leon-Berman

Photography by Galdones Photography

Library of Congress Cataloging-in-Publication Data

Names: Williamson, Brooke, author. | Goode, JJ, author.
Title: Sun-kissed cooking : vegetables front and center / Brooke Williamson with JJ Goode ; photography by Huge Galdones.
Description: First edition. | New York, NY : Harper, an imprint of HarperCollinsPublishers, [2024] | Includes index. |
Identifiers: LCCN 2024013419 (print) | LCCN 2024013420 (ebook) | ISBN 9780063333796 (hardcover) | ISBN 9780063333802 (ebook)
Subjects: LCSH: Cooking. | Cooking (Natural foods) | LCGFT: Cookbooks.
Classification: LCC TX714 .W5245 2024 (print) | LCC TX714 (ebook) | DDC 641.6/5--dc23/eng/20240327
LC record available at https://lccn.loc.gov/2024013419
LC ebook record available at https://lccn.loc.gov/2024013420

24 25 26 27 28 TC 10 9 8 7 6 5 4 3 2 1

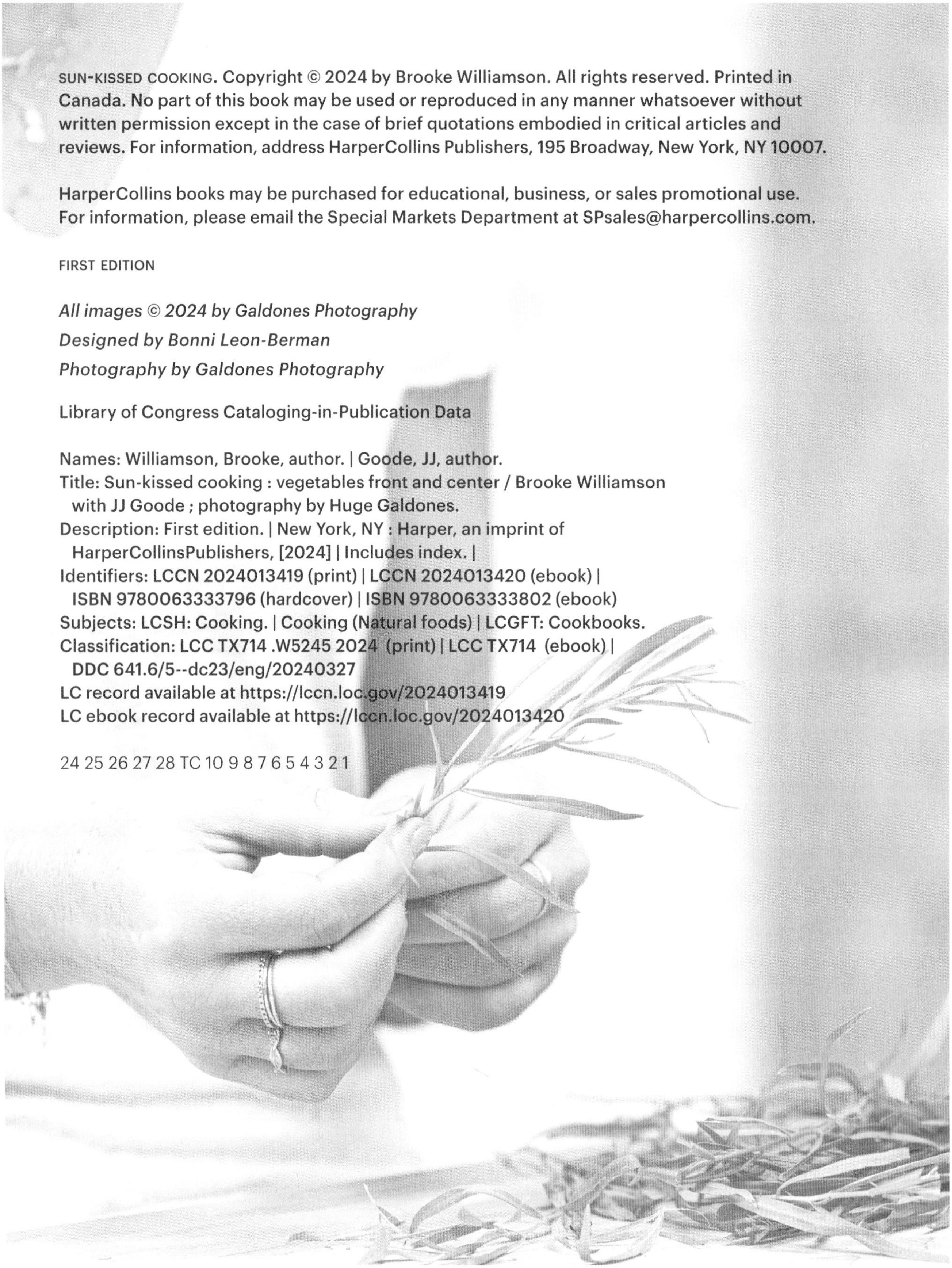